A Cage Called Hope

NATIONAL
LIBRARY
OF AUSTRALIA

A catalogue record for this work is available from the National Library of Australia

www.adelaideanxietytherapy.com
Murphy, Shelley (author)
A Cage Called Hope
ISBN 978-1-922527-15-8
Self-help

Cover and book design by Green Hill Publishing

A Cage Called Hope

Hoping till it hurts and beyond.

Become the person you want to be

Not

The person you were programmed to be.

Shelley Murphy

Mum: no longer at my side, forever in my heart
My brother Mike, proud and strong; you proved them wrong
My daughter Lisa, you rose above it all,
strong, resilient and full of love
My son-in-law Dave, you are a blessing
My clients, it is an honour to walk beside you

And then there is
Brendon the private man who has supported me
Intellectually, emotionally, physically and
spiritually for the past 30 years
Showing me that I deserved all of that and then some
Teaching me my dreams were far more than dreaming
My partner in practice; my partner in life

You have my heart and my gratitude

Contents

Contents

Foreword

WHO IS THIS BOOK FOR?

If you think the following:

- There is something wrong with you.
- The quality of your life and relationships is not providing a return equal to your efforts.
- "Bad things" keep happening.
- You never feel good enough, attractive enough, successful enough, or loved enough.
- You feel responsible for how others behave.

Despite all the evidence that points to it being time to change tactics, you refuse to give up. You get up each morning with a heart filled with fresh hope. You don't know how to do it differently.

- You are tired, but not defeated.
- You feel weak, but you are incredibly strong.

This book is for the strong, the resilient, the brave.

Yes, you!

This book is to help you stop repeating the same old patterns, expecting a different outcome. This book is to show you the real reason why hope is not enough and why you haven't been able to get to where you so desperately want to be (and it has nothing to do with you not being good enough!).

This book is about setting you free from the cage called Hope. Freeing you to be the person you want to be, not the person you were programmed to be.

You will learn about the secret saboteurs—core beliefs—and how to change your relationship with them. You will find your authentic self within these pages and the courage to live your life unapologetically, should you choose to do so.

I have been blessed to work with many people from all walks of life. It's the most rewarding experience to work with someone, hand them the tools they need to let go of the shackles of the past and watch them grow into lives they believed they didn't deserve. The answers can be found in our childhoods because that is where our core beliefs are formed. Some are better than others and it is possible to identify the ones that are holding us back so we can create positive change in our lives.

This book is for all of us, no matter our family of origin. For those confused by living in two conflicting worlds: professional success and personal mess. We will often hear "but I had a great childhood" and I am not here to convince you otherwise. What I am proposing is if your life is not going in the direction of your choosing, there is a good chance you have a core belief that is working against you.

It is for all of us who unintentionally set up ourselves to fail because of the impossibly high standards we set for ourselves and others. It is for all of us who strive to love and be loved; no matter how hard we "work it", we are unable to give ourselves permission to stop, even in the face of the countless reasons we should.

If you read this book and become motivated to change that which doesn't support the creation of the life you want, then my job is done. If you read this book and it confirms for you that you are living your best life, then my job is also done.

You will get the most out of this book if you are prepared to read with an open mind. Please know that what is written here is done so with no judgement, so there is no need for defensiveness. All of us—no matter what hat we wear—share similar experiences.

At the end of the day, this is my opinion based on my personal and professional experience; you can choose to do with it what you will. A little tip: if your buttons are being pushed and you are having an intense emotional reaction, there is a clue that you might want to spend some time there (or not).

We all get up in the morning filled with good intentions. If good intentions are not creating the outcomes you want, I suspect that you have been using the wrong kind of Hope. The type created based on lies, sitting silently in your subconscious and unintentionally undermining your conscious choices. The good news is that with awareness, motivation, and willingness to get a little uncomfortable, you have the power to get where you want to be. And you don't have to do this alone, either—I will be right by your side the whole time.

Perhaps I have piqued your curiosity enough that you will join me on this journey.

Welcome

I AM SO PLEASED YOU FOUND me. Your choice of reading material gives me more than a hint about how you are feeling. I know there is a part of you buried deep within that hurts like hell. I know you are exhausted, confused and your optimism is leaking from you at an alarming rate. I know that each night, you put your head on your pillow feeling like you have nothing left; each morning, you get up with a heart filled with fresh hope, convincing yourself today, somehow, will be different.

Up until now, you have been caught up in a cycle of promising, committing, and disappointing yourself time and time again. You believe yourself to be powerless to break this repetitive cycle. You are convinced you are a failure. Your self-talk is unkind and cruel and, frankly, unhelpful. The way you talk to yourself is a very important clue as to why you feel unable to stop. So, my newfound friend ,we need to look at that horrible self-talk of yours.

Despite what you believe about yourself, you are not stupid. You are not going crazy. You are a victim of your own core beliefs. Stick with me, friend. I will show you that not only is it possible to break free from who you were programmed to be, but you can become the person you have been striving to be. You have been trying to do this on your own, but you can relax now; you have found your tribe. There are a lot of us out there.

Now is the time to stop hoping and start living. Yes, it is noble to aspire to be a good human. However, the pursuit of this doesn't require the surrendering of your safety, self-respect, confidence or your mental and physical health! If it has, you have lost your way, friend. Any relationship—I will say that again, *any relationship*—that requires you to be abused to any degree is either a relationship that needs a makeover or a relationship that needs to be abandoned. I will show you how to tell the difference.

As a counsellor, a statement I have heard many times is, "Well, that's easy for you to say. You haven't had a life like mine". I don't take that personally because it is one hundred percent correct. I don't know what it's like to be you but, just like you and everyone else, I've had my own stuff to work through. I am not ashamed to admit that I have been guilty of dancing too long with hope and working too hard to be loved. I have also had the experience of releasing myself from core beliefs that held me back and impacted the quality of my life and relationships. I know how fantastic it felt—and continues to feel—to free myself of burdens that were simply not mine to carry. It felt so good I wanted to shout it from the rooftops but I'm not that good with heights, so I chose another route.

With the benefit of hindsight, I would say that my experience in all likelihood motivated my unconscious choice of career. I have been fortunate to work with beautiful souls from all walks of life. Their stories are varied, but there is one common thread: core beliefs causing harm in their lives, ranging from existential angst to homelessness, addiction and beyond. I have seen it all. I will never tire of this work. How could I? I witness transformation after transformation as my clients grow beyond crippling core beliefs.

I have experience needing to be loving, kind, and forgiving way beyond the point of reasonableness. My inexhaustible capacity to hope became a cage; invisible to the naked eye, unavailable to the human touch, it stood between me and the quality relationships my heart ached for. The irony is I had the key the whole time.

Love is essential for humans to thrive. Our wellbeing depends upon it. We leave the womb seeking reassurance that we are loved and safe. Defenseless and extremely vulnerable, it is essential to our survival that we receive the love we seek. Our initial reception and our subsequent childhood experiences cause us to form a unique set of beliefs about what the world thinks of us, what we can expect, and how we should navigate it. Some of us will get the golden ticket and know that we were loved and always will be. Some of us will have circumstances thrown at us that will cause us to seriously doubt that. Some of us will learn that we are not lovable despite the best efforts of our caregivers. It is this "not good enough" belief that fills us with shame and sets us on a quest to earn that love. Until we can get that love, we will fill the void with hope.

If we grow into adulthood with a belief that we are unlovable, then it wouldn't seem logical that we could arrive at a place of loving ourselves. Instead, we are filled with shame and will do everything possible to make sure that our defectiveness remains unseen by others. We will do our best to camouflage our shame by building outwardly successful lives. We become the high achievers, the people pleasers unable to keep still for too long in case our secret is uncovered. After all, it is harder to hit a moving target, right? For some, the burden will be so great they will find themselves on the pathway to self-destruction. The pain is so great that they unconsciously self-medicate by choosing substances, relationships, and lifestyles that threaten to end their lives, silently seeking an end to the pain they can't understand.

I will not lie to you. I respect you and your strength far too much. At times, this will not be an easy ride. You will find it a challenge. You will want to defend yourself, your choices, your relationships, and whatever else is painful to look at. That is all part of the process; if there was a short cut, I would let you know, but the only way is through. I am asking you to commit to reading with an open mind, to getting a little uncomfortable, so you can jump off the merry-go-round. Why? Because you are worth it!

I have every confidence that if you open up to the possibility after our time together, you will know it also. You are far stronger, resilient, and capable than you believe. I know that because you are here. Despite everything that has happened to you and because of you, my friend, you are still standing. You are still breathing, You are still seeking. You are still loving. You will need to look back, yes, but only for a moment and only to find the clues to effect real change.

Memories and emotions will come up. Memory is a shadow of the initial experience. You have already been through that challenge and you survived. How do I know that? Because you are here. You are strong. It has taken real strength to get where you are and that same strength will see you through these pages. The difference is that you will come out the other side changed in ways you never imagined possible and in the ways that you have chosen.

Unlike the events which made you doubt your value and strength, this situation is radically different. This time, you are in control; you get to choose the pace that you move. This time, you are not alone. I am right by your side.

Purpose

"The most terrifying thing is to accept oneself completely"

- C.G. Jung

AM PREPARED TO BE OPEN about aspects of my journey to demonstrate none of us get through this life without being challenged in some way. I am not saying it is easy. When we are trying to make sense of those challenges, we wish for an easier life. I like to believe if we are prepared to embrace the struggle, we will come through the other side a far better version of ourselves than we could have imagined. When I was going through a particular moment in my life, I found inspiration in the Parable of the Butterfly. This is a summary.

A man had been watching a butterfly for hours as it was trying to emerge from its cocoon. In all that time, it had only made the smallest of holes and the body of the butterfly was simply too large to get through it. The butterfly had grown still from exhaustion. The man was kind-hearted and couldn't bear to see the butterfly suffer any longer. He used scissors to cut open the cocoon and release the butterfly. The butterfly was free, but its body was very small and its wings were not fully formed. Watching and hoping that the butterfly would open its wings and fly away, the man was disappointed. Nothing happened. His action motivated by kindness meant the butterfly would never fly. It would live out the rest of its life with a shrunken body and wings incapable of flight. The kind man didn't realise it was the struggle to get out of the cocoon that enabled the butterfly to fly.

This book is not autobiographical, even though I will reference personal experience. My disclosures are for demonstration. These will be easily identifiable as "I" speak. A great deal will be written in "we" speak, referring to the experience of being human. The "we" voice is a constructed voice comprised of personal and professional experience, my clients, and my training. This isn't intended to be an academic piece of writing intended to impress you with psychological jargon and theories (the libraries are overflowing with those). I want to start a conversation that will leave you confident that you are no longer alone—that somebody out there gets it and, more importantly, gets you.

Separation is an illusion. We are all connected by the shared experience of being human. Individuals such as yourself can give up the unconscious patterns of behaviour that make you feel so lonely and misunderstood. This new understanding will make it possible for you to break free from the chains of the past so you can evolve into your best self. Your evolution benefits not only you, the individual, but ripples are felt throughout our families, workplaces, and the community at large.

If you know something is missing but you still don't know what, ask yourself the following questions. If you find yourself answering "no" to any of them, that's a great place to start.

- Do my relationships nurture me?
- Is my job fulfilling?
- Am I living life with integrity, honesty, and good conscience?
- Am I contributing to the world by being of service to others?
- Am I happy about the quality of connection with family and friends which include safe physical contact?
- Do I have a hobby or sports which I am passionate about?
- Do I engage in activities that feed my soul?
- Is my sex life working for me?

The reasons we continue doing the things we don't want to be doing are powerful, rarely discussed (unless you are in my line of business) and go by the name of core beliefs, which are primarily formed in childhood. Some core beliefs are good, some are not so good and some need to be thrown out.

If you have some core beliefs that aren't working for you, it doesn't necessarily mean that you had a bad childhood. You can form faulty core beliefs in any childhood. Our childhoods don't have to be perfect for us to have a good chance of growing up into well-adjusted adults. We can also grow up with some problem areas and still have reasonably successful relationships with others. It all boils down to the stage of our brain development at the time the core belief was formed and the intensity of the emotion we were feeling.

The struggles we experience in our adult relationships are often a reflection of how we feel about ourselves. The clue that we may have some work to do on the relationship with moi is when we find ourselves inexplicably going, doing, and being in ways we have consciously decided we no longer wish to behave.

As these core beliefs and the relationship with ourselves are formed in childhood, it is helpful to understand a little more about the important elements for childhood development. There is a huge difference between surviving and thriving and this is no different for children. To thrive, these six essential criteria must be met:

- Basic safety
- Connection to others
- Autonomy
- Self esteem
- Self-expression
- Realistic limits

If these needs are not met in childhood, we will experience sadness, anger and fear. The sadness is a consequence of our needs being neglected or unfulfilled, combined with anger at those who failed to meet our needs. This leads to the birth of a fear in adulthood that we may never find a partner who can be there for us.

Children need a stable and secure family environment. You note the words "stable" and "secure", not perfect. The key to stability is primary caregivers who are consistently available both physically and emotionally. When we experience neglect and abuse in childhood, this lack of safety will lead to an adult who is unable to trust. If you couldn't trust and relax around the people meant to care for you, how are you to feel safe in the world?

Love, attention, empathy, respect, affection, understanding and guidance are essential if a child is to grow beyond basic survival. A child needs balance in all areas of their life. Some of you will resist the idea of looking at your childhood and I get that. The reason I am starting with childhood is that we all have one; it is a vital time regarding the development of our core beliefs and the formation of subsequent value sets.

This is not a witch hunt. This is not an opportunity to lay all blame at the feet of parents. Parents (I sincerely believe) become parents with the best of intentions. Far too often, those intentions are derailed by circumstances beyond their control. Maybe there was a death in the family, perhaps a divorce. Maybe Mum was admitted to hospital for an extended stay due to an unexpected illness, you were sent to boarding school or you had to be put into care for a while. Maybe you were raised by the nanny or grandparents because your parents were busy building the family fortune, maybe one or both of your parents had a problem with drinking or drugs, and maybe your parents fought constantly and you thought that they were going to divorce or kill each other. Maybe things changed for you when your siblings were born or you were so valued that you were totally overprotected and you simply didn't learn how to navigate the world. These maybes don't change that none of that was your fault.

Phew! That is one long list of maybes and you know what? There are many, many more where they came from. What

I am trying to point out is that life happens despite our best-laid plans and intentions. When it happens, it can have unexpected consequences not only for the adults but also for the children sitting in the midst of it all. This, however, does *not* absolve the parents of the responsibility they have. We must establish context.

Let me repeat: *this is not a witch hunt*. You can have the best family in the best house on the best street in the best city, leading what you believe to be the best life, and then "stuff happens". Everyone will be scrambling trying to put family life back together in a way that makes sense, but the solutions found may not seem at all logical to children. Children are not grown-ups; they will be limited in their capacity to understand the bigger picture. It is the need to make sense of these circumstances to feel safe once again that triggers the formation of core beliefs. This helps provide a sense of control in a world where, because they are children, they have no control. Children are reliant on their parents to teach them the meaning of the world around them. It is this reliance that elevates parents in their children's eyes as God-like figures: all-powerful, almighty, and all protecting.

We are born with two fears: the fear of loud noises and the fear of falling. These are evolutionary in origin, hard-wired in our brains to ensure our survival. All other fears are taught. The intensity of the emotions that we experience at the time of learning will wire the brain so we can avoid the situation in the future.

Many of us will grow to adulthood with the fear of not being good enough. Because of their stage of brain development, children are literal. If we have done well and get praised, we interpret that as being loved. If we have been caught doing something which hasn't pleased the adults in our lives, we will believe that love is being taken away. We are little puppy dogs seeking pats on the head. Not many parents were taught how to distinguish between the child's behaviour and the child when they are giving feedback; they are not conscious of the need to modify their language to reflect the difference between the person and the action. The praise or punishment isn't attributed to the action but the person as a whole. The "good girl" or "good boy" enthusiastically awarded makes a child feel ten feet tall (*I am loved, I am loved*). "You bad girl" or "you bad boy" fills a child with shame (*I am unloved, I am unloved*). Good is the goal because that means you are lovable and, well, you know what that makes the other.

It is expected that parents have the capacity and skill set to love their children unconditionally and have the maturity to see their children as individuals, not as an extension of themselves. Many a poet has written of the purity of a mother or father's love, which for many feels like an impossible benchmark. No one points out how difficult stepping into aspiration-filled slippers is. The harsh reality of realising the honour of parents can be very different from what we imagine because no one can teach what they don't know.

The following are some reasons why some parents have difficulty in demonstrating love appropriately, even if they have the best intentions:

- They have no self-esteem and hold a low opinion of themselves
- They have been immature themselves on becoming a parent and weren't prepared for the enormity of the job
- Their own childhood has left them uncomfortable with or unable to accept unconditional love
- They have unresolved trauma
- Becoming a parent has reminded them of their mortality and it frightens them
- They view their children as their "legacy" as extensions of themselves and their unrealised aspirations
- They see their children as possessions and confuse this with love
- They don't have adequate parenting skills and don't like the way their children behave, even if they have caused the issue
- They struggle to like or love their children

There is no parent training college. Parents are trained to be parents by their parents. The "training" is their childhood. Some of us will be destined to repeat the family pattern of parenting. Some of us, because of the intensity of certain experiences, will parent in a different way to what we experienced in our childhood. The point is that our childhoods will influence the way we parent. We will unconsciously recreate, repeat, or react to our child's self-understanding of our childhood.

If we are amongst the lucky and have managed to reach adulthood, we all share the same legacy: to overcome the pain created by our childhoods, whether intentional or unintentional. By stepping up to the challenge, you make a difference not only in yourself but for future generations of your family. Only through positive action can we break the patterns of the past; depending on an over-reliance on hope will ultimately result in selective blindness to protect us from the truth of our imperfect childhoods.

As adults, we have a luxury available to us that wasn't available to our child selves. We have the luxury of choice. We can choose to be a victim to the past or we can choose to write a new story: the story of us. Not the story of other's opinions of us, not the story of our value being determined by the flaws of others, and certainly not the story we have maintained for so long by patching with hope.

- We can choose to bust out of our cage which our hope has created for us.
- We can choose to be who we want to be not who we were programmed to be.
- We can choose to unapologetically claim our magnificence and live our lives.
- We can choose to grow up and understand the difference between a reason and an excuse.
- We can choose to look objectively at the truth and grow beyond it.

Are you ready to give yourself the love you always deserved and have been desperately seeking from others? Are you ready to surrender your story of how things should have been, accept that all parties did the best they could—which may or may not have been good enough—and step truly into adulthood?

Whether your answer is a resounding "Yes!", a timid "... Maybe" or a defensive "Get stuffed!", you are in the driver's seat, maybe for the first time in your life. You and only you can choose to turn the page (or slide right, if you have an ebook).

No matter what you choose, I will be there.

E-motion

"When we are no longer able to change a situation,
we are challenged to change ourselves"
—Viktor E. Frankl

PHEW! SO GLAD YOU ARE here. I acknowledge at this point I may have stirred up a variety of reactions.

Some will feel deeply defensive, some will be vaguely curious about my intended destination, some will be feeling the stirrings of connection and for some, you will be hoping that this is going to go somewhere but be experiencing the uneasy feeling that it probably isn't. Others will be thinking that they have already gone too far; they have invested five minutes of their life reading this, so there is no point in turning back now. All of the above doesn't surprise me at all.

Many of us live our lives that way with the "Oh well I've gone this far" mindset. Some of us even do so when we can see we are heading for trouble; we just hope this time will be miraculously different. We are so creative in ways to avoid the truth that we start to believe our modified version and become so convinced we expect others to view our circumstances in the same way.

This is particularly true when it comes to our relationships. We can't see what we could see if it was someone else's relationship. The reason we can do this is that there is no pay-off in deceiving ourselves. However, in our relationships, we are not able to achieve that level of objectivity.

For the demonstration, let me introduce you to our hypothetical couple. Partner A insists on choosing outfits for Partner B. They are unable to leave the house if Partner B has selected the outfit. Partner B doesn't recognise this as controlling behaviour. Partner B's friends have commented on the behaviour with a degree of concern. Partner B has not taken on board their concern, even though it is not a good idea to go against the selection and wear something different because Partner A will sulk and refuse to go out. What then happens is because somebody in the circle of Partner B's friends/family/colleagues draws attention to the behaviour of Partner A, Partner B becomes uncomfortable; their carefully-constructed reality is being challenged. Partner B needs to believe that Partner A is demonstrating love and care for them and facing the truth of what is happening is far too painful. The need to defend this point of view is so compelling that Partner B is more likely to end contact with friends/family/colleagues rather than raise the subject with Partner A.

There are a couple of things going on here. This course of action (or non-action) can be attributed in part to the psychological phenomenon unique to humans known as "sunk costs". A classic example of this is gambling. Rational human beings will throw good money after bad because they hope that the next race will be the magic race that will pay off. We continue with a course of action simply because of the time we have invested.

Time is valuable and the need not to waste it will see us commit to "seeing it out" even in the poorest of choices.

This may bring up for you another human protective mechanism called denial. You might be saying out loud (or in your inside voice), "Nobody does that!" Really? To which I will now respond, "Yes! People do that stuff!" Have you watched a movie to the very end, even though you hated it? Me too! Hope holds you in that seat, waiting for that magic moment when the movie redeems itself and turns into the movie you dreamed it would be! That is the behaviour of sunk costs, which you may or may not be acting out now.

I ask you to persevere because, unlike gambling, you are not required to throw more money at it to see it through. Unlike the movie, you won't end up with no feeling in your backside and covered in popcorn. There is a very real possibility that the instinct that made you pick this book will pay off. This is one time where the phenomenon of sunk costs will have a positive outcome. That in itself is worth a little more of your time, isn't it?

Emotions: we all have them. We also have certain emotions that we do our best to avoid. These are the emotions we have been trained to believe are bad, which has lead to some confusion regarding the purpose of emotions.

Emotion is simply e-motion = energy in motion. A feedback mechanism to let us know how we are doing at that moment. Is life working or not working for us at this moment? Am I safe? Is there something I need to be doing? Nothing more.

Emotions, whether we want to feel them or not, all have an important part to play.

- **Fear** is the energy of judgement, allowing us to become aware of and identify danger zones when we are trying to get our basic needs met.
- **Sadness** is the energy of goodbyes through our lives. We will continually say goodbye to the ending of our cycles of growth.
- **Grief** is the energy that, when combined with sadness, assists with closure and completion of the past.
- **Guilt** is the energy which forms our conscience.
- **Shame** is the energy that reflects to us our imperfections and motivates us to seek help.
- **Happiness** is the energy that lets us know that all our needs are being filled. We are becoming and growing.

One of the primary emotions which motivate us to lean on hope is fear. It is such a big contributor it gets to be in the spotlight for a moment—only a moment, because we humans tend to spend a little too much time there and it doesn't lead us to happy places. Five significant fears can be formed in childhood:

1. Fear of abandonment

We all have a fear of this to some degree. This fear is not only about partners or friends, but also family members, pets, or even those with whom we don't have a very strong bond.

This dependency is formed from a fear of rejection. People with this fear have experienced abandonment as a child, whether accidentally or intentionally.

2. Fear of rejection

This isn't isolated to the rejection by others, but also applies to the rejection of self. The fear can begin in a variety of ways involving rejection from parents, family, friends, or siblings. We interpret this as being unlovable because, at that moment, we feel unloved.

3. Fear of humiliation

This occurs when we have been parented by highly critical, extremely strict, and disapproving parents. You would have had criticisms such as, "You are so clumsy, bad, immature, annoying, etc.". Self-esteem cannot thrive under such a constant barrage of negativity.

4. Fear of betrayal

This is born because our parents didn't deliver on their promises. As a result, we develop mistrust, jealousy; the relationships we build are not healthy.

5. Fear of injustice

This is born from having parents who were emotionally distant and authoritative. As the demands are extreme and allow little margin for error, we are up for failure as it is asking the impossible.

The following breakdowns of FEAR helped me keep me on track when I was going through my metamorphosis:

FEAR AKA **False Evidence Appearing Real**
FEAR AKA **Frightened of Emotions so Avoid Reality**

Hope can become toxic when motivated by fear. The fear of the truth of our reality. Humans are the masters of avoidance, especially of all things we find painful. We pack it away in a way that we can't do with our fears. What makes it even more intense is that we humans have so much fear and it comes in all sorts of shapes and sizes! Fear of not fitting in, fear of not being lovable, fear of not having the perfect family or perfect partner—fear, fear, and more fear! We are a walking, talking festival of fear. It is the intensity of these fears which keep us invested in false hope.

Fear and the routines we create to avoid those fears will become automatic. We live our lives responding unconsciously to our fears, trapping ourselves in a cage we have unconsciously created because of our need to feel safe. We lose the sense of who we are. Our lives become one long Groundhog Day as we run straight toward the precipice that we have plummeted over countless times before.

The overarching fear for many is not being loved and not finding the perfect partner. We unrealistically hope that there is one person, friend, or partner who will meet all your needs, make you feel good about yourself, and maintain you in bliss-filled happiness. Society supports this faulty notion that we need to be completed by another human to arrive at a place called "happiness".

This is a lie, people! The essential elements for good relationships are two whole (not incomplete, not parts thereof) people who choose to be in the relationship not because they need the other to "complete them", but because they are complete, happy in their skin, happy with their own company and have love to give. When you come into a relationship with the mindset that the other party is going to compensate for the holes you feel in your soul, it is destined for failure. You are asking to be rescued, not to be loved. That is not sustainable and accounts for why you believe you have been unlucky in love when it has been neediness that has sabotaged you. We will get into that more later.

We all want and desire. Our choices in response to those wants and desire both unconsciously and consciously shape our reality and subsequent quality of life. Investment in avoidance of the "e-motions" that we are not comfortable with or have labelled as bad is not a wise investment. The avoidance stops us from creating the life that we desire.

Humans hold within us such great potential and are more powerful than we believe or have been taught to believe. We have the power to imagine, to dream, to be inspired, and to be creative. This is only possible if we are in an environment that supports the personal freedom to know, feel, imagine, decide, and love appropriate to our age and development.

The very foundation for how we feel, talk and think about ourselves begins forming from the time we draw our first breath. Some say even earlier. I believe that each of us—no matter what we have begun to believe or have been taught—are all unique and precious. If we are unable to believe that about ourselves, then something has gone awry. The fear you are stuck with should not be believed.

Cages

I T'S TIME TO TALK ABOUT cages and why I am using it as a metaphor. Please tell me that you have not reached this stage of the book under the impression that it is a book on welding cages! I am referring to the limits that we impose upon ourselves for a variety of reasons. So for all you welders out there, I guess this is where we say goodbye, unless you have decided to go with the flow and stick around. If that's the case, the more the merrier!

The fear that drives the need to protect ourselves from the truth is so seductive that we begin to believe it to be the truth instead of recognising it for what it is: a fear built based on a faulty core belief. In our desire to feel safe, connected, and loved, we will relentlessly pursue hope. Instead of creating the safety we crave, we have inadvertently made ourselves more vulnerable.

Although invisible to ourselves and the world, these cages are no less restrictive than cages of the more traditional kind.

Eventually, it will come to our awareness that we have been living life behind bars because aspects of our lives are so damn uncomfortable and the pain of not changing exceeds the pain of remaining in our cage.

I am speaking from experience. I have seen the movie, read the book, and have the T-shirt. My cage was called Hope and it was built on the core belief that I wasn't good enough. Over time, the bars were strengthened by things intangible to the naked eye such as serial forgiveness, excuse-making for those who hurt me, consoling those who mistreated me, apologising for myself, my actions, and every other thing I mistakenly believed that I had influence over.

I had a chip on my shoulder and this in turn stoked the fire burning in my belly. Without a hint of self-awareness, I was driven by a need to prove I could do whatever any male could do—if possible, I would do it better. I was huffing and puffing so you couldn't see my fear.

My father was killed in a workplace accident when I was nearly three years old. No need to bore you with the details, other than the trauma caused a core belief to be formed: the people I love will leave. My father "left" and my brain made sense of it the best way it could at my stage of development, concluding that there must be something wrong with me. Emotion is the anchor for the formation of the core belief. So long story short, I was experiencing a terrible feeling. My brain decided it didn't like that feeling; thus, a core belief was formed to "protect" me, causing me to act in ways that would prevent me from experiencing that pain again. Perfect sense!

The memory of being abandoned—or, more accurately, the feelings I experienced when remembering being abandoned— were so horrible that the very thought that it could happen again frightened me. The fear was real and had very real impacts on how I responded to the world. How I felt about myself shifted moment by moment based on how others responded to me and the meaning I read into those responses or lack thereof. In the space of a day, I could emotionally buffet between soaring like an eagle and singing the "Nobody Loves Me, Everybody Hates Me" song as I reacted to my perception of how people felt about me. My ability to perceive what was going on around me was always clouded, as I read every situation through the filter of my "not good enough" core belief created when I was just a baby.

Until the age of twelve, I was a chronic sleepwalker and was plagued by nightmares. I would dread going to sleep. Without fail, I would shut my eyes and there it was—in 3D, surround sound, the same old terrifying nightmare. It haunted me for the longest time. So much so that, up until about the age of ten, I would also wet the bed. The intensity of emotion I experienced all those years ago has burned the memory into my brain, occasionally drifting into consciousness. Thank goodness there is no longer emotion accompanying any recollection; however, what I do remember is the meaning I took from the dream. I understood that I wasn't afraid of dying as my father had. What I feared intensely was being the one left behind, abandoned and alone.

The Nightmare

T WAS ALWAYS ME ON a yacht, at night, stormy seas
all by myself.

The waves, watery skyscrapers

The sky almost black

A scrap of moonlight

Rudderless with no means to steer, buffeted by howling winds

The wind so cold freezing my blood

The waves, coal-black, doing their best to feed me to the
hungry ocean

Arms straining, holding the mast in a desperate embrace

Cold and terrified

Screams for help swallowed by howling winds

No one could hear me; no one could see me, no one to save me.

Alone

Y TWO-YEAR-OLD SELF MADE SENSE of our family's tragic loss within the limits of my brain development. Not having the capacity to understand death, all that I would have known is that my father was there one minute and not the next. My father abandoned me and it must have been something I had done or hadn't done (child understanding). My understanding of death at this age would be that it was temporary and reversible. I also would not have understood that I could die. Dead people and animals are broken and can be fixed, or they are asleep and can be woken or they can come back. It is no wonder that I would interpret my father's death as an abandonment.

I formed the belief that the way to keep people in my life was to be better than the rest (am I the only one who heard Tina Turner?). I became hyper-vigilant, attempting to read and predict the needs of the people around me. I made sure that whatever I did, I did it well; if I thought I couldn't, I would refuse to participate. My professional self recognises this as a classic abandonment pattern and the perfectionism that grew in response to that. Unfortunately, quite a few decades had to pass and a lot of tears cried before I attained that level of wisdom!

"When unresolved issues are writing our life story, we are not our autobiographers; we are merely recorders of how the past continues, often without awareness, to intrude upon our present experience and shape our future directions"

— Dan Siegel MD

Humans create meaning through stories. We teach with stories. We process our experiences using story. During our lives, we will amass many stories (memories). We come unstuck when we select one story out of all the stories available to us to identify with. This story we hold onto is bookmarked by the intensity of the emotion we experienced at the time. My grief at the unexpected departure from my life by my father lead me to build my "not good enough" story.

Some of those stories will have a happy ending and lead us to believe good things about ourselves and some will impact us negatively; they are the ones without a happy ending. The emotional pain associated with that story will blind us to all other perspectives. It is this limited view that will form the foundation on which we shape our values and our personality.

The catalyst for the birth of an "I am not good enough" story in childhood is usually traumatic, caused by circumstances outside of our control—unexpected, beyond our comprehension, something which happened to us or because of us, not created by us—and yet we interpret this powerlessness as a deficiency in us. The sudden death of my father and the stage of my brain development caused my child self to believe that if I had been good enough, he would have stuck around. This set the tone for my belief in how the world would treat me.

A child's ability to make sense of the world is limited to their stage of brain development. Everything is reduced to a comprehension of the black and white kind. Good things happen to good people and bad things happen to bad people and every thought we think must be believed. Of the tens of thousands of thoughts we have in the day, the majority are incorrect and the rest are repetitive negative loops. This unconscious acceptance of this bullshit (therapeutic term) creates a world of pain that outlasts the memory of the event that set all of this in motion.

That is why you will hear people refer to themselves in terms of their experiences: "I'm bipolar", "I'm a survivor", "I'm a junkie", "I'm a Mother", "I'm a sex abuse survivor", "I'm a Counsellor"—the list goes on. We absorb the things we do or the challenges we have faced as the definition of who we are. We are so caught up in the emotion of the experience we overlook that we are a human being having those experiences. We then set on a course determined by the unconscious selection of people/experiences/situations based on who we believe ourselves to be as a consequence of the events we have experienced in our lives.

I will continually remind you that these core beliefs were formed by a child. We then walk through life wearing our story/

core belief like a name tag at a conference: "Hi! I am a victim. I am damaged/broken/incomplete. I am a survivor", or whatever story you have adopted to define you. As a child, whenever asked to talk about myself, I would promptly respond with, "My dad died when I was two". The older I became, the more detailed the story became; I would attach the latest terrible thing that had happened in a never-ending sequence of tragedy. By the time I was thirty, I had a list as long as my arm of "shit" things that happened to me and the new expansion pack of "I don't understand why, because I am a good person?"

Surprise, surprise: those terrible things kept on coming because I had a core belief that was what I deserved. What I wasn't conscious of was that I was seeking approval, validation, sympathy—anything that would give me respite from the suffering created by my "I am not good enough" story. Unfortunately, external validation is in direct contradiction to what you believe to be true about yourself. At best, it gives you temporary respite; at worst, it locks you into repeating the same old choices, reinforcing the story you hold as true.

Our stories formed at such a young age amid terrible trauma will create memories full of inaccuracies and assumptions, padded out with third-party perceptions. Stories are repeated in families. One version is accepted as the absolute truth (a version dictated by the adults in the house) and eventually, your version of events blurs into the agreed family consensus because we are creatures wired for survival. This can lead to confusion and causes us to lose trust in ourselves.

The consequences of being confined to cages of the invisible kind are little different from their more traditional counterparts. I think it is far crueller because you have no awareness of the self-imposed restrictions you are living within. A caged animal can at least see the bars; just like you, they may have no understanding of how they got there, but at least they have visibility of what is between them and the freedom they crave. Should the animal run at the bars and collide with them, they can connect the dots and work out that the lumps of metal probably had something to do with the throbbing pain in their shoulder. It is not that obvious with cages made of hope. We can spend decades throwing ourselves at those invisible bars; it hurts like hell and we will have no idea where the pain is coming from.

I know exactly what that feels like. Blissfully ignorant and fatally optimistic by nature, I kept running headlong into those bars! I kept going around in circles, becoming increasingly confused by my successes in some areas of my life and feeling like a total failure in others. My capacity for "goodness" seemed to increase the burden of the expectations of myself and others. I couldn't shake the feeling that I was an imposter, even though I was living an outwardly successful life.

Knocked repeatedly (and painfully) onto my ass, I never gave up. Failure was not an option. Not sure why I was so driven but convinced that one day my efforts would pay off, I was ignorant to the price that I was paying. My determination was something that I was extremely proud of.

Five little words changed all of that. Five little words took away the blindness and stripped me of the complicated layers I had constructed to avoid looking at the truth of how little I valued myself. Five little words woke me to the reality that I had been living in a cage. A cage built from good intentions. A cage called Hope.

Those life-changing words were small in stature, but large on impact: *Hope is not a strategy.*

What is Hope?

"PANDORA BROUGHT THE BOX OF ills and opened it. It was the gift of the gods to men, outwardly a beautiful and seductive gift, and called the Casket of Happiness. Out of it flew all the evils, living winged creatures, thence they now circulate and do men injury day and night. One single evil had not yet escaped from the box, and by the will of Zeus Pandora closed the lid and it remained within. Now forever man has the casket of happiness in his house and thinks he holds a great treasure; it is at his disposal, he stretches out his hand for it whenever he desires; for he does not know the box which Pandora brought was the casket of evil, and he believes the ill which remains within to be the greatest blessing, it is hope. Zeus did not wish man, however much he might be tormented by the other evils, to fling away his life, but to go on letting himself be tormented again and again. *Therefore he gives Man hope, in reality, it is the worst of all evils, because it prolongs the torments of Man.*"

— Frederick Nietzche (Human All Too Human, 71. Hope)

I am open to the possibility that after our brief time together, you may have concluded that I am anti-hope. That isn't the case at all. I am pro- the kind of hope that is helpful and anti- the kind of hope that erodes your confidence and self-esteem. Hope, like ice cream, is available in different varieties.

Hope, may be one of the three theological virtues; however, there are dangerous aspects born from hope when it has been misdirected and misplaced. It holds the potential to solidify our attachments to people and places that are destructive to us. It is this phenomenon that I am referring to when I talk about the stuff that cages are made of.

Let's go back to basics and begin with an old fashioned dictionary definition of hope. The basic definition strips away the romance, mythology, personal interpretations, denial, and any form of self-deception:

hope

noun

The expectation and desire for a particular thing to happen.

Synonyms: pipe dream, daydream, dream, aspiration, wish, desire, expectation, ambition, plan.

verb

Wanting something to happen or wanting something to be the case.

I'm hoping for an apology

Synonyms: expecting, wanting, waiting for, being hopeful, pinning your hopes on, or anticipating.

So how does the act of hoping get so complicated? What the dictionary offers is a view just of the tip of the iceberg. Beneath this definition lies the complex layers created by us humans. This shouldn't be surprising to you—we do tend to complicate things. Our thoughts and emotions complicate the act of hoping, especially when it is hope born from hurt and further complicated by a fear of being hurt even more.

The dictionary is in the business of providing definitions. It doesn't (nor should it) offer guidelines regarding time limits for hoping or identify the signs of hope becoming hopeless. It doesn't reveal the secret that it is possible to hope until you hurt and when you wake up to what you are doing stopping is permissible.

Hope as a topic of discussion is not new. Alexander Pope spoke of man's unique relationship with hope in his poem "An Essay on Man" (1733). Human beings are wired to hope for the best even in the face of adversity and to hang on at all costs is considered an honourable course of action. I am not disagreeing with Mr. Pope and I don't wish to disrespect him; I just believe there is a "but" that needs to be addressed here. It is one thing to soldier on in the face of adversity and a different animal to continue to hope when all the signs indicate that you have no hope of achieving your goal. Especially when that hope is based on the belief that your behaviour can influence others to make different choices about the way they respond to you.

I have no doubt hope enhances the quality of our lives. Hope can be the salve when applied to our lives in appropriate doses. Hope has the potential to ease our emotional, spiritual, and physical wounds. Hope can provide a much needed soft place to land.

- Hope can fill the calm before the storm.
- Hope can be the rock that we cling to during turmoil.
- Hope can keep us afloat.
- Hope can fill the chasm that waiting creates.
- Hope can walk beside you when the solitude is too vast to navigate alone.
- Hope can be your mantra in the toughest of times.
- Hope can inspire to try "one more time"
- Hope can feed our tired minds and motivate our exhausted bodies.
- Hope can manifest the seemingly impossible.
- Hope can encourage us to work towards goals even in the face of adversity.
- Hope can be the answer.
- Hope enriches our humanity

Hope, I believe, is the feeling equivalent of the multi-purpose, get you out of any situation Swiss Army knife. What this knife can do is limited only by the user's imagination, just like our friend Hope. Hope is very useful. It keeps our mind nice and optimistic based on our expectation that there is the possibility of a positive outcome. Hope is not unlike a public swimming pool in the middle of a heatwave; it may appear overcrowded, but somehow there is always room for more.

If I am such a pro-hoper, how on earth do I find myself starting a discussion that includes hope, cages, and harm in the same sentence? I suspect that at the very least it makes me sound confused and at the worst... well, it's ok. You can say it: a little unbalanced. I believe knowledge is power, which compels me to discuss the not often talked about other side of hope that has the potential to trap you.

Hope is born from desire and shouldn't be confused with expectation. If all you have is the desire or goal, you don't have enough. You need to assess, plan, and act; when you have done all that you physically can, then comes the time for hope. Nothing can be achieved by sitting, moping, and hoping.

The truth is that if we just hope and nothing else, there is a very real possibility that we will become anxious and depressed because we won't achieve our goals. It is harsh, but wishing doesn't get results; neither does hoping without doing. For healthy hope to exist, we need to have exhausted the options available to us. The rest, as they say, "is left in the lap of the gods".

Unlike the hope based on the likelihood of success, false hope harms our wellbeing. Our feelings of confusion, isolation, and exclusion from the happy lives that we believe everybody else has continues to spiral out of control. So we repeat the cycle. Try, cry, repeat. Our lack of progress confuses us as we sincerely believe being good is enough to have our hopes fulfilled.

The confusion is more of a metaphysical giddiness caused by the constantly spinning in ever-increasing circles as we try to satisfy the insatiable hunger of our "not good enough" monster. This monster is nothing more than an unwanted squatter occupying our minds and decimating our increasingly-fragile egos. We lose sight of what we are doing and why we are doing it.

Not all core beliefs are faulty and not all hope is toxic. However, core beliefs that are born from the belief that you are not enough and you have to compensate for that will make you extremely susceptible to forming a dependence on false hope. The hope of the false kind is addictive because it provides a protective buffer between you and the truth of your relationships with self and others. Hope is destructive when it leads you to make well-intentioned choices that cost you. They cost you your self-esteem, quality of life, quality of your relationships with yourself and others, career progression, creativity, mental and physical health, love life, sex life—YOUR LIFE.

If we hold the core belief that we are fundamentally flawed and we have to work hard not to have our awful secret discovered, we will never find peace or balance. Like a duck on the water, we will look peaceful and calm above the waterline whilst our little legs are working like crazy just to keep us afloat.

We are all born with the right to be loved and protected—no exceptions. That is the truth. Unfortunately, we are born into imperfect families created by imperfect human beings within the context of an imperfect world, and the way we interpret our situation can lead us to the mistaken belief that we are the cause for those imperfections. This can make you feel incredibly isolated but trust me, you are not alone. Those core beliefs created by the juvenile brain can be reviewed and updated, making them fit for purpose. They are not meant to be life sentences.

"The pendulum of the mind alternates between sense and nonsense, not between right and wrong"

— Carl Jung

You simply didn't know what you didn't know. The core beliefs unchallenged will become self-fulfilling prophecies. You will make choices and wear the consequences of those choices, which will later be interpreted as evidence of the truth of your core belief. This is not a bad thing if you believe that you are a collection of all things amazing but alas, far too often that is not the case. If you believed you were good enough, you would not need to devalue yourself to earn love. It is usually the old chestnuts such as, "I'm not good enough", "I'm unlovable", "People like me don't get to...".

Our tribe's focus after our arrival in the world is getting us feeding, walking, talking and all the rest of the fundamentals we humans need for survival. Nobody is thinking we might have to discuss the formation of core beliefs at some stage. They may not even know they exist; chances are that no one had the core belief chat with them either. Let's face it: most of us got to adulthood without the sex talk, so we made it up as we went along. Not much different, really.

As an adult, there are opportunities available to you that weren't there as a child. You are no longer living in the same set of circumstances, so it makes sense to upgrade those core beliefs. You can choose to live your life less reactively because you are all grown up. I know that it may be difficult to believe, especially when you go to your parents for a family lunch. As soon as you walk through the door you are teleported to the age of five again, inexplicably acting in ways that are unconsciously motivated—especially if your siblings are at the table as well. It is "game on Donkey Kong", with everybody slipping into their child roles competing for approval from Mum and Dad. We can't help but to unconsciously fall into the same dysfunctional patterns that maintain the family model by everybody adopting their designated roles.

Yes, you will always carry aspects of that child within you. However, it is no longer appropriate for your child self to be making big operational decisions. It is downright unsafe and at the very lowest intensity will get in the way of you realising your true potential. Your child self needs to be relegated to the stakeholder and your adult self needs to accept the role of CEO. Quite frankly, your child self will be happy to hand over the burden— especially if it was in charge for as long as I suspect it has! It is time to separate yourself from your parents and stand on your own two feet, creating a new relationship consisting of equal adults. This is essential if you don't wish to unconsciously slip into the parenting patterns of the past.

When we are continually repeating the same behaviour hoping for a different outcome, it is usually is motivated by love. We are trying to earn love, hold onto love, feel loved, or fall in love.

We are seeking approval from our families, friends, work colleagues, or lovers. When the people we target our efforts on don't respond in the way we would like or fail to notice, we assume the responsibility for their reactions (or lack of). We conclude we haven't tried hard enough, been enough. Our response is to dance the same dance we have always danced since we were children.

Try, cry, repeat.

"No matter how beautiful you make it,
a cage is still a cage"
— Mahrukh

Deception

*"Because true belonging only happens when
we present our authentic, imperfect selves to
the world, our sense of belonging can never be
greater than our level of self-acceptance"*
— Brene Brown

AT TIMES—AND ESPECIALLY WITH CERTAIN people—we can be pretty slow to recognise we are being lied to. We find it even more difficult to identify the lies we tell ourselves. Our ability to see is clouded by our desperation to be perceived as perfect or to have our version of the truth mirrored back to us. We lose objectivity and we confuse desire with reality as we unconsciously bend the truth. We not only deceive ourselves but become convinced that others will see what we see. The mind helps us with our deception. It has this neat little trick where it reacts with the same emotions whether we are having the experience, remembering the experience, or imagining the experience. We feel it, we think it and then believe it.

Our desire to be loved and the way we earn it is based on a core belief formed in childhood. If our childhood experiences haven't been consistent or positive and are scarred by trauma, what we have learned about ourselves and love are highly unlikely to be factual. Because of their stage of brain development, most children interpret love as conditional. It is seen as a reward for good behaviour and is just as easily rescinded when our behaviour is perceived as bad by the caregivers responsible for turning us into "good" people.

It is only natural that parents want their children to become successful, represent the family in the best light and, above all, fit in. Many of us are not taught how to love ourselves or exposed to the possibility. This is partially due to parents' concern that they will somehow raise an overly-confident child who believes they are better than everybody else. Unfortunately, some of them did too good a job in that department and the only time we can feel good about ourselves is when we receive approval from others.

Our ability to make conscious choices will be constantly undermined by what we do not know: the core belief sitting in the subconscious. Our inability to meet the goals set by our conscious minds because they conflict with the core belief will be perceived as a failure on our part and interpreted as evidence that the core belief is indeed right.

Emotional reactions are stored as memories in the amygdala structure in the limbic systems of the brain. We react with shame, which is very different from guilt. Guilt says "My behaviour is wrong. I take responsibility for my behaviour, I apologise and I will address that behaviour". Shame says "There is no separation between my behaviour and myself; if my behaviour is wrong, then I am wrong. I can't change who I am, so I must be unlovable. I must work harder to win you over".

"Shame is the most powerful, master emotion.
It's the fear that we're not good enough"

— Brene Brown

This is just a small list of ways we project what we think others need to see and hear to seek approval. In our quest to hide our shame, we find ourselves with a real conflict between what we say publicly and what is happening privately.

Please believe	Reality
"I hardly eat a thing."	I can't stop binging and I feel ashamed
"I rarely drink."	Less than a bottle a night and I feel ashamed
"I live for my family."	Sometimes I resent that and I feel ashamed
"They are just being protective."	I feel smothered and I feel guilty about that
"No thanks. I don't dance."	I'd love to but I am scared of being judged
"I speak my mind."	I get flooded by emotion when I think I am not being heard
"I love football, soccer, movies, etc. etc."	I hate them all but if I don't say I do you won't spend time with me
"I just love doing things for people."	Sometimes I wish someone would love helping me but I can't accept offers of help

"I can cope."	I need help but I am unable to ask for it
"I am the go-to person in a crisis."	Other people's problems distract me from my reality

This is just a very small sample of the unconscious self-deception that we humans use to save face and the discovery of our shame. The lies we choose will depend very much on the core beliefs that were formed in our childhood. These core beliefs determine our personalities and values. See if you can find yourself in the following list. Don't stress if you find more than one pattern—that is not uncommon.

Perfectionist:
Goals: Transparency and truthfulness
Belief: To be loved, I must be good and right
I am proud to be: Conscientious, Always focused on improving, Responsible
I am ashamed that I can be: Critical, Self-judging, Resentful

Partner:
Goals: Influence
Belief: I must give fully to others to be loved
I am proud to be: Relationship-focused, Supportive, Caring, Helpful
I am ashamed that I can be: Demanding, Meddling, Pushy, Arrogant

Self-starter:

Focus: Getting results

Belief: I must achieve and accomplish to be loved

I am proud to be: Efficient, Fast-paced, Goal-focused, Hard worker

I am ashamed that I can be: Impatient, Image-motivated, Inattentive to feelings

Authority:

Focus: To be the cream of the crop

Belief: I must have and maintain the "perfect" relationship to be loved

I am proud to be: Authentic to self, Empathetic, Idealistic

I am ashamed that I can be: Moody, Self-absorbed, Dramatic

Analyst:

Focus: Technical knowledge

Belief: I must protect myself from a world that gives too little and demands too much

I am proud to be: Analytical, Thoughtful, Seeks self-sufficiency, Non-demanding

I am ashamed that I can be: Overly private, Detached, Withholding

Worrywart:

Focus: To question everything and accept nothing on face value alone

Belief: I can't trust the world, so I need protection and security
I am proud to be: Curious, Friendly, Honest, Dependable
I am ashamed that I can be: Fearful, Critical, Overly doubtful

The Appreciator:

Focus: A new opportunity
Belief: Life must always be up and open for it to be a good one
I am proud to be: Adventurous, Pleasure-seeking, Upbeat, Optimistic
I am ashamed that I can be: Self-serving, Uncommitted, Avoidant

The Head Honcho:

Focus: All or nothing
Belief: The world is tough, so I must be strong and powerful to protect myself
I am proud to be: Action-oriented, Strong, Justice seeker
I am ashamed that I can be: Impulsive, Excessive, Overbearing

The Negotiator:

Focus: Minimise conflict
Belief: I must blend in and get along with everyone to be loved
I am proud to be: Comfortable, Steady, Harmony seeking, Self-forgetting
I ashamed that I can be: Stubborn, Avoidant of conflict at all costs

Monsters

SOME WILL DEDICATE A WHOLE life to hoping and cry often because it hasn't changed a damn thing. Hope is a lot of things, but it is not a magic pill. Hope that is not supported by action rarely gets results and will often end in tears. Contrary to popular opinion, it is not enough to recite the magic mantra, "I hope it all works out". There is a time and place for the mantra, and that is after we have done all we can. Those things include actions of a practical nature: goal setting, connecting with people who can advise/guide/teach you, setting timelines/milestones so we have a real chance of gaining what we have hoped for. Alas (I just love that word— I wish I could use it more often). Alas (yes, I just did just because I can), unlike Dorothy, we have to do far more than click the heels of our ruby slippers to see our hopes come to fruition.

I previously mentioned the other side of hope. We tend to deal with it the same way we "dealt" with the monster that lived under our bed when we were children. You know, *that* monster: the one that taunted you every night, robbing you of sleep no matter how hard you hoped it would just disappear, forcing you to creep into your parents' room only to be told yet again to "stop being silly". Each time, as you were left to the lonely walk of shame back to your room, you would become desperate. You decided to face your fear and check out the underneath of your bed (prime territory for a monster lair). Surprise! No monster! Filled with disbelief, you hypothesised that it had relocated to another child's bed; maybe it picked up on your newfound fearlessness and ran for its life. For a moment, you considered that the monster had been a figment of your imagination. How could it have felt so real?

What we imagine often does. Remember that old brain thing? You know, sending the same messages to our body, regardless of whether it's a remembered, real, or imagined experience.

The "Monster" side of hope is when we are convinced that mindlessly repeating the same old behaviour will deliver a different outcome. I know, I know: we have all heard the definition of insanity. It also can be a sign of good-old-fashioned avoidance (aka false hope). Avoidance is not the easy option; the pain is real as you lock yourself into a repetitive cycle of "Try, cry, repeat".

I have to call it as it is. This is a toxic kind of hope that, although pure in intention, causes us to stay in harmful situations (psychologically, spiritually, emotionally, and physically) far too long and erodes our self-esteem. Situations that, if we weren't busy being so damn hopeful, we would immediately recognise as places we have outgrown and have no business being in.

The reasons for hanging on to hope too long are different for every person, but the shared origin is childhood. All good stories have a protagonist and a villain, the one that causes hurt and chaos in the lives of the characters we love. Toxic hope is the villain in our story. Just like in the movies, the good guy needs to dig deep to find the strength they didn't realise they had and discover that the bad guy can be put in its place.

Hope is often used to manipulate the unsuspecting. It is more than likely that you have witnessed Person A deliberately giving Person B false hope by convincing them that their wishes will come true—not because they want to see Person B happy, but because Person A has something to gain.

Let's take the hypothetical situation of a boss with a dedicated employee who, quite frankly, does the work of three people. The business's productivity is directly attributable to the efforts of this person. They have been open and honest about their professional goals, informing the boss that they want to climb the corporate ladder. The employee hopes that their goal can be achieved within their current workplace; however, they have declared that if there is no opportunity for promotion, they will move elsewhere. The boss is horrified by this, as they know that the employee would leave a great hole in their organisation. What the boss also knows that the likelihood of promotion within the organisation is close to none. This is a real ethical dilemma: does the boss put his business at risk or tell the truth?

The boss decides not to declare this piece of important information because of their needs and the needs of the business. The boss dangles the carrot of hope: there is nothing available at the moment, but the employee will be the first to be considered if a role were to open. The employee feels flattered and assumes that they will not have to move to fulfil their corporate goals. The boss has deliberately held back information to maintain the status quo and the employee now has a hope that is not based on the truth. This is manipulation.

Giving false hope can also be motivated by the need to protect someone we care about from being hurt or disappointed. Again, we have seen many examples of this in life. How many times have you heard mothers pad out the truth so that their child doesn't have to deal with the truth of why another adult has let them down?

We "protect" ourselves in the same way, except the dialogue is internal and unconscious. What we think, we accept as fact. We lovingly lie to ourselves and give ourselves false hope. Lying by omission consciously or otherwise doesn't change the fact that it is indeed a lie. The layers of self-protection and self-deception are so complex, so intricate and so convoluted, that we have no awareness of the motivation for our actions or the cause of our uneasiness. At times, we will have moments of uneasiness regarding our behaviour/talk/self-talk, which we instinctively repress.

We repeat what we want to believe to be true over and over again. We take exception to people who attempt to point out the incongruences in our lives. Remember our employee with the manipulative boss? A friend might suggest that the boss isn't being honest and the employee will be offended by that suggestion, or feel the need to defend their honour. Why? The employee wants to believe what the boss is saying; they want to believe that they are valued and hope that their dream will happen. To challenge this would be the end of hope. The employee admitting they have been conned will lose face and feel foolish. The truth of the situation is so confronting that there is a very real possibility that the employee will choose to remain with the boss and let go of their friend despite the facts.

Holding on to false hope and the choices we make to support that hope causes harm. Harm to our self-esteem, our quality of life, our ability to trust in ourselves, and our relationships with ourselves and others. The extent of that harm is determined by the strength of our denial.

- False Hope holds us in loveless relationships.
- False Hope retains abusive people in our lives.
- False Hope encourages us to trust others before they have earned it.
- False Hope causes us to ignore or discount our safety.
- False Hope erodes personal boundaries or convinces us that such boundaries are unnecessary.
- False Hope demands we place all others before ourselves, no matter the personal cost.
- False Hope turns us into doormats, thanking those that wipe their feet upon us.
- False Hope robs us of our voice.

- False Hope deceives us into believing that even if we do not value ourselves, others will validate us.
- False Hope convinces us that this time, they meant sorry and they won't repeat the behaviour.
- False Hope leads us to believe that if we are patient enough, justice will prevail.
- False Hope tells us that we can drink, eat, and self-medicate enough to bury the pain for good.
- False Hope convinces us that love conquers all, even abuse from family members.
- False Hope leads to perfectionism.
- False Hope leads to denial.
- False Hope tells us that *the one* will complete us.
- False Hope thinks someone else can take our pain away.
- False Hope tells us that, if you work hard and long enough, no one will discover our imperfections.
- False Hope believes if we suppress our needs, others will respect us in the way that we can't respect ourselves.
- False Hope tells us that we will finally feel safe around people who are not safe to be around.
- False Hope tells us that we can forgive ourselves for not being lovable enough.
- False Hope tells us there is truth in our fabrications, delusions, and eternal optimism, even though we don't believe it ourselves.
- False Hope believes that doing more of the same will result in a different outcome.

· False Hope leads to believing that one day, we feel
  lovable and loved.

Core Beliefs

"Until you make the unconscious conscious,
it will direct your life, and you will call it fate"
— Carl Jung

SHAME AND A DYSFUNCTIONAL RELATION-
SHIP with hope are the fruit of the seeds planted during
childhood. Simmering in our subconscious, they will influence our entire lives until they are bought to awareness and
challenged. At the time, they were created to keep us safe. Our
caregivers were gods to us—the beginning, middle, and end of
our universes—because of our total dependence upon them.
Without them, survival wasn't guaranteed. We made sense of
the world in the best way we could within the limits of our development. Unfortunately, we were surrounded by often distracted adults who didn't fully comprehend the responsibility
that came with our vulnerability.

This is not the green light to wave your finger at your
dysfunctional family. My experience leads me to say with confidence that because families are comprised of imperfect humans,
the odds of being a part of a "perfect family" are against you.

Professionally, I've not encountered any. I'm not saying they don't exist, but they don't tend to come to therapy. I also have never encountered parents who became parents to pay forward the pain of their past.

The truth is that the caregivers and adults we had contact with during our childhoods may have been ignorant of the impact their actions (or non-actions) had upon us. That doesn't mean they didn't care. Quite frankly, they were in all likelihood distracted by all that living a grown-up life entails. If they had been blessed with a high level of self-awareness of their short-comings as a parent, many would have felt powerless to change their behaviour. For some, this is the case because of an irresist-ible compulsion to repeat the past. For change to happen, you need to be aware that change is needed and to release the layers of protection you have accumulated over a lifetime.

What I do know from my personal and professional experience is that parents—whether they become parents through clever planning or by accident—never become parents to mess up. Even the parent guilty of the grossest negligence will likely proclaim love and devotion to their children. Does that mean that they knew how to love their children safely? Not necessarily. Does that absolve them from the responsibility of caring for their children properly? Short answer: NO. That may be the reason for their behaviour, but it doesn't excuse them from the consequences of and the subsequent responsibility for changing their behaviour.

With families comes history, and that history creates legacies. Some of these legacies were dark and sinister; some of them not so much. Some of these were simply out of the control of the adults in our lives, such as death, homelessness, unemployment, trauma, poverty—the list is as long and diverse as the human experience itself. No end of situations can test and stress the family unit. In the midst of it all are vulnerable children, trying to get their needs met and driven by the need to survive.

Caregivers teach the children the meaning of the world around them. In response to what is being shown to them, they will develop core beliefs about how the world will treat them, the quality of relationships they deserve, as well as their capacity, capabilities and talents. Children are doing this at a time when their brain is wired to think magically, non-logically and egocentrically. Their mind is immature and unable to differentiate from the objects and people around them. Therefore, the child's viewpoint—according to the child experiencing it—is the only viewpoint. It is not easy being a parent; it is not possible to get it right all of the time, although we are burdened with the expectation that we will and can.

Types of harm that can cause childhood wounds and outcomes in adulthood

Childhood experience	Adult legacy
I was yelled at, hit, or exposed to violence.	I am afraid of people's anger.
I was judged harshly and frequently.	I feel inadequate and bad about myself.
My boundaries were violated. I was intruded on, smothered, or abused.	I don't know how to reclaim my boundaries.

I was dominated and controlled.	I don't like it, but I allow people to control me. If it feels like it is happening again, I run.
I was exploited. My parents saw me as a way to meet their needs.	I feel I have to be doing something for people to want me in their lives.
I trusted a caregiver and they betrayed me.	It is hard to trust anyone.
I was constantly made to feel guilty.	I am unable to forgive myself.
I reached out for a connection and was dismissed.	I don't expect people to like or want me.
I wasn't adequately nurtured or cared for.	I feel empty and needy.
I had no consistent care. My caregivers changed, got divorced, or there was a death in the family. I felt abandoned.	I am scared to love because I might be left again.
I was not seen or appreciated.	I feel invisible in my relationships.
Bad things happened.	I feel flawed and people will find that out about me.
Because of what happened to me, I'm not lovable.	I believe I am not lovable.

In fairness, parents are no different to the rest of us mere mortals; one does not know what one does not know. Also being a mere mortal, we simply can't be objective in the midst of the subjective experience. Humans see what we believe. The irony is that in a world where one is required to be trained and licensed to operate machinery, all you need to become a parent is a functioning set of reproductive organs.

That is why so many parents get caught up in trying to correct their childhoods through their children. They are motivated not to make the same mistakes their parents made or experience the poverty, divorce, natural disasters, etc that befell their parents. Even if you are choosing positive things in reaction to a not so positive childhood, you are still being controlled by your past.

Unfortunately, what is also missed is that children are not smaller versions of their parents. A child's needs and wants are unique to themselves. They are not cardboard cutouts or an opportunity to heal the injustices of a parent's childhood. So even if we are successful in creating the childhood that we dreamed of for our children, we may have—for all the best reasons and with the best of intentions—created a childhood that they will busily try to rectify for their children.

Parents aren't perfect. Even if that was possible and we could be raised in a utopian reality, there would just be something else that would cause issues for us. The family unit will always be faced with challenges—that's called life. We don't grow up in bubbles. There will always be influences from external sources that are outside of the family's control. It is through exposure to those elements that we grow up to be resilient. We also need to understand that it is okay to take charge of our own lives when we become adults. It is essential for healthy development that we differentiate from our family of origin.

"It is a healthy approach not to expect persons to turn out precisely how you would have wished"

— Criss Jami

A core belief is a shortcut, not unlike a shortcut on your computer. When we create a shortcut, it is to save time: with just one click, you can get to a programme you use regularly or that assignment you have been working on. It's a time saver because you are not required to repeat all the steps to open that particular file. You click on the icon and the shortcut takes all the steps to get to the programme that you want to open. Your subconscious operates in a similar way. It stores all the information (the steps on how to get there) and has developed a shortcut (core belief/ neural pathway) so that there is no need for thinking. No remembering—just the required file opening up when faced with a triggering set of circumstances that create the emotion in question.

Remember learning to drive? At first, the amount of detail we had to attend to was overwhelming, intimidating, and frightening—and that was just putting the key in the ignition! So we practiced. The repetition installed a shortcut so it was no longer necessary to be conscious of every step. Our actions become automatic, so much so it becomes possible to travel our normal route often enough (work, school) to arrive at our destination with no recollection of the journey at all! Driving has become a part of our routine, so there is no need for conscious thinking. The only time we snap out of it and pay attention to what's happening is when something out of the ordinary happens, like a dog running onto the road, roadworks, or a change in the speed limit.

Core beliefs are reinforced by repetition and the intensity of emotion connected to the experience. That is why some people may decide they can't drive at all if they had a fright as a learner driver (which may or may not include a hysterical parent in the passenger seat). The decision is made ("I can't drive") and the memory of the incident reinforces this belief because of all the emotion flooding in to accompany it. These "bookmarks" set by emotion cause us to respond in unconscious ways to certain situations. For example, our person who adamantly believes they cannot drive a car may be a passenger with someone else at the wheel. The driver barely misses a dog that has run onto the road into the path of the car. Brakes screech and the collision is avoided. Everyone is safe; however, the passenger is a shaking mess and has no conscious idea why.

The hint that we may have a core belief that conflicts with our conscious choices are the repetition of behavioural patterns that we have identified as unhelpful. We repeat situations/relationships/experiences that create our pain and are genuinely surprised that we have done it again, berating ourselves as "stupid", "useless", or "brainless" for having no control or discipline.

When we finally tire of this self-defeating behaviour, we can open up to the possibility that we need to learn a new strategy as it is now painfully clear that we are unable to change by repeating the same patterns. This unfamiliar territory will need to be approached with bravery, commitment and an understanding that it will be uncomfortable to start with. The alternative is to stick to what you know; seeing as you are here, my guess is that it hasn't been working too well for you.

The Mind

"Our subconscious minds have no sense of humour, play no jokes, and cannot tell the difference between reality and an imagined thought or image. What we continually think about eventually will manifest in our lives"
— Robert Collier

KNOW IT IS HARD TO swallow that the beliefs that we hold about ourselves are formed at such a young age. This is a natural response because we humans need to believe that we are logical, practical, solution-focused, conscious, and in control of our reality. Nice to think, but the problem is that is not how we are designed. Being in conscious thinking mode only five percent of the time is a rather clever brain adaptation that, to put it in complicated scientific terms, stops our heads from exploding. A little melodramatic, I admit, but it did get your attention.

We are learning machines. From the moment of our birth, our brains are absorbing, adapting, and growing. This can be directly attributed to the brainwave state that we are in as children. Brainwaves are patterns of electrical activity occurring in the brain. They are crucial to all aspects of brain functioning:

thoughts, emotions, and behaviours. We have five different brain wave states:

- **Delta:** The slowest brainwaves, generated when we are meditating or in dreamless sleep. This is our primary brain state from the age of zero to two. At this level, there is very little critical thinking or judgement taking place. Whilst in the womb, we receive our programming in this state; this is how babies learn to copy a smile, etc.

- **Theta:** Also occurring in sleep and relaxation, this is a state of inner focus, dreams, and vivid imagery. This is the predominant state for children two to six years old. Unable to show critical or rational thinking, this is the brain state of dreaming and imagination. This is the super learning brain state; children are highly suggestible and will accept what you tell them to be the truth. People who are in a hypnosis-induced trance are in this brain state.

- **Alpha:** These waves occur in our quiet thoughtful times when the brain is resting. Children from five to eight years old start to form their analytical mind; they will interpret and draw conclusions from the world around them. However, their inner world of imagination is experienced as equally real as the outside world.

- **Beta:** Our normal waking state, the world of conscious analytical thinking. We are alert and focused on problem-solving. We move into this stage from eight to thirteen years. This brain state is where most of us adults hang out.

· **Gamma:** These are the fastest waves associated with higher levels of consciousness.

Zero to six years is a crucial time to build positive beliefs for children; any messages received will be interpreted as true because they haven't yet formed conscious analytical thinking. A belief is born from thought. That thought is rehearsed until it becomes a belief.

Repetition trains the brain and creates shortcuts with the sole purpose to ensure that we can carry out everyday tasks without bringing them to our conscious mind. Walking, talking, singing, dancing, setting the table or putting a spoon in our mouths are examples of the many, many things we do daily without engaging in conscious thinking. If we were to bring all the elements of all the activities that we carry out every single day to conscious thought, we would be overwhelmed. If we broke down each activity into individual elements, we would be surprised by their complexity. It would be like doing it for the first time every time we attempted it.

Walking, for example, is something that (if we are lucky) we get to take for granted daily. There are many steps involved in the action of walking that we were consciously and painfully aware of when we first learned how to walk. Let's take a trip down memory lane and try to break down the act of walking into individual elements:

· **One:** Relax shoulders and keep them back and down.

- **Two:** Stand tall with a slightly lifted chest and a straight back.
- **Three:** Bend arms ninety degrees at the elbow and swing in time with the opposite leg. This balances the body.
- **Four:** Point chin down and pull in slightly to place the neck in a neutral position. This supports the head and prevents neck pain.
- **Five:** Check hips are level and that your knees are pointing forwards. Keep pelvis tucked under the torso.
- **Six:** Check steps are equal length.
- **Seven:** Don't tilt your head to one side—hold it straight.
- **Eight:** Don't slump your shoulders.
- **Nine:** Don't strike the ground with your toe first. Use your heel, feel the pressure roll towards balls of your feet, then push off your toes.
- **Ten:** Oh and don't forget to keep all your support functions going at the same time—breathing, seeing, sensing, etc.

As a how-to, I am aware that there will be glaring omissions for some and not enough detail for others. The point is that activity we take for granted and perform countless times in our lives is engaged in with no conscious awareness of how we are doing it. This is possible because of the comprehensive information stored in our subconscious; therefore, no conscious thought is required for us to walk successfully. The decisions about when to walk, where to walk, things to avoid when walking or what weather to walk in is all stored in the subconscious, so our choices are pre-programmed based on our collective experience and the emotion it evoked at the time we were experiencing it. That's why some of us LOVE walking in the rain, some HATE it and some are neutral. If walking in the rain was a special time with a loved one, we may be programmed to enjoy the experience. If you slipped and fell, breaking your leg, you may not be wanting to repeat that experience and will automatically avoid it.

Take a moment to reflect on how tiring it would be to consciously think about every little step of all the complicated things we do in a day: driving the car, grooming, work, even relaxation! We wouldn't get anything done! The only time we have to dedicate thought towards an action is when we are learning that new skill. Once we have the skill committed to memory and those lovely neural pathways are built, the subconscious takes over. The subconscious is a huge memory bank that is largely taken for granted. It holds in storage every detail of your life so far and will retrieve that data as needed. Its key function is to ensure that everything you say and do is in line with what you have been programmed to believe about yourself.

So in short, that means that *ninety-five percent* of brain activity is beyond conscious awareness. This ninety-five percent is responsible for controlling drives, impulses, fears, instincts, emotions, and automatic behaviours. It is this part of your mind that operates without any awareness or control on your part.

The subconscious is also responsible for homeostasis: maintaining body temperature, keeping you breathing and your heart beating at a certain rate. Using your automatic nervous system, it maintains a balance among the hundreds of chemicals in your billions of cells. It manages to keep your entire physical machine running in total harmony most of the time. I don't know about you, but that impresses the hell out of me.

The subconscious mind is also responsible for maintaining homeostasis in your world. Its role is to ensure that your thoughts and actions remain consistent with what you have said and done in the past. It knows we feel best when we are operating in our comfort zone. Every habit you have formed over your life—be it good or bad—is memorised by your subconscious. It works hard to keep you in them, even if they are destructive.

One way the subconscious lets us know that we have deviated from our comfort zone is the experience of emotional and physical discomfort when attempting anything new or different. It automatically defends against our attempts to change the established patterns of behaviour. Even the thought of doing something new will create feelings of uneasiness and tension. This is because many core beliefs are held together by unprocessed emotions; when we identify a belief, bringing it to the conscious, the corresponding emotion arises as well. When this happens, we often retreat because we are surprised by the emotion or we don't want to feel it. We are quite delusional when we talk about mind control because, in reality, we are being subconsciously controlled and we have no awareness of it. When we become aware, however, it is possible to update the core belief or remove it by processing the emotions. The relief that follows will lead you to feel lighter and happier.

Let's recap: we use our conscious mind just five percent of the time and it is this area of the brain that is responsible for logic, reasoning, creativity, and will. We also have another state of mind that steps into action when we are stressed. Stress is the body's way of getting you to return to the state of homeostasis and, when triggered, it kicks your "analytical mind" into gear. Some of you may have noticed that when you become stressed, you overthink things.

We operate from our subconscious mind ninety five percent of the time and it holds our:

· Skills
· Habits
· Emotional reactions
· Hardwired behaviours
· Conditioned responses
· Associative memories
· Routine thoughts and feelings
· Attitudes
· Beliefs
· Perceptions

Explicit memories such as knowledge and experience are seated in the conscious mind. Implicit memories are held within the subconscious, as well as subconscious states, repeated experiences, and emotional reactions. The body becomes conditioned to the mind. You have practiced these patterns, yet you have no recollection of why or how you do what you do. The emotions attached to these memories are so powerful that they anchor you to the past and create your personality. Your personality is how you think, act, and feel; that personality then creates your reality. How you think, act, and feel about you, the world, and others are formed as core beliefs in your childhood. There it is! We have just come full circle.

Core beliefs which bind you to the type of hope that hurts

There is something wrong with me	I'm a loser/stupid/bad Everyone else is better than me I can't do anything right
I am unlovable	I'm unwanted It's easier to be alone Nobody gets me/Everybody hates me I'm better off flying solo
If I love someone they will leave me	Everyone leaves me It's unsafe to love anyone If I love you, you will hurt me I have to earn love I can only be happy when I have a partner
The world is a dangerous place	Nothing/no one can be trusted You are all out to get me I have no power/I'm helpless and weak Control will guarantee my survival I must always be on guard and never vulnerable Keep who you are to yourself

I am not good enough	I am what I am
	People like me don't succeed
	I can't
	Everyone else is better than me
	Always the bridesmaid never the bride
	What's the point in trying?
I'm different/ an outsider	I don't belong
	It's like I'm an alien
	I can't be understood
	There's something wrong with me
	I can't show who I am; they won't like me
I have to be happy to be liked/loved	If I do bad things, I am a bad person
	It is wrong to have bad thoughts
	I can't be angry because you won't love me
	I can't be sad because you won't like me
	I don't want to feel my feelings

Everything is my fault	I'm never right
	I need to try harder
	If I love them enough, they will change
	I have no choice—I have to help
	It is selfish to think about my needs
	I can't be anything less than perfect
I'm special	Nothing but the best for me
	Look at me, look at me
	There is something wrong with you if you criticise me
	I'm better than you/I have to be the best
	The rules don't apply to me
	People don't get me
	I can't get it wrong

A trigger is an experience that takes place in the here and now which unexpectedly takes you back to the past. We find ourselves immersed in the old feelings and compelled to act out in old ways because of the anchoring emotion attached to our painful core belief. They "pop up" in everyday situations. For example, you may have had a controlling parent and now you are all grown up and earning your dollars but find it a real struggle being told what to do. You are very reactive to the way you are asked to do things, often being accused of overreacting and acting in ways that have the potential to sabotage your career. This is a classic example of a trigger.

Emotional triggers which could also apply to this imagined scenario are:

- Being asked to do something you don't want to do
- Taking orders from authority figures
- Having somebody else control you
- Lacking confidence or feeling judged as not good enough
- Thinking errors (remember: just because you think it doesn't make it truth)

With awareness and understanding of the root cause of our triggers, we can then choose our actions/reactions to circumstances and cease living our lives like someone else is holding the remote control. It is possible to recover from being unexpectedly triggered and overwhelmed by the accompanying emotion. It is possible to actively shift your emotional state.

You can practice this step at any time, even when you first notice a reaction, to help you think through your triggers and responses. When you determine what you want to do next, shift into the emotion that will help you get the best results.

- **Relax** – breathe and release the tension in your body.
- **Detach** – clear your mind of all thoughts.
- **Centre** – drop your awareness to the centre of your body just below your navel.
- **Focus** – choose one keyword that represents how you want to feel in this moment. Breathe in the word and allow yourself to feel the shift.

Stop trying to manage your emotions. Accept that you can't stop them from arising, don't label them as good or bad, and don't resist. Instead, choose to feel something different when an emotion arises that you don't want to be overwhelmed by. Notice it, accept it, observe it, learn from it, and let it go. Then make choices that will generate the emotion you want to be feeling at that moment. So it could go like this:

"Oh, I'm feeling really sad (*noticing*). That's ok—sad can't hurt me (*accepting*). Why am I feeling this way? (*observing*) Mmmm... it reminded me of the way X talked to me (*learning*). Well, X isn't in my life anymore and that's a good thing (*letting go*). I am so happy that the whole relationship is behind me! (*choosing*).

This is how we begin to behave our way into emotional freedom.

We All Have a History

"The most fundamental harm we can do ourselves is to remain ignorant by not having the courage and the respect to look at ourselves honestly and gently"

— **Pema Chodron**

N THE INTEREST OF HELPING others to build a safer relationship with hope, I am going to share my story. I believe it is the right choice; however, I admit I am a little nervous. Why? There is a small part of me that thinks that you may judge me and not respect me. After all, I am a *professional*—do you not expect me to soar above human frailties? "Is it a bird? Is it a plane? No, it's Super-therapist!" Well, I don't wear my underpants on the outside and I don't have superpowers (except for the standard-issue that comes with being human). Truth is, I now respect myself too much to try and convince anyone that I am perfect and in my honesty, I am demonstrating my respect for you and permitting you to be imperfect too. I want you to know that you are not alone; you are not the first to fall victim to "hanging in there" for too long. There is life on the other side.

So what came first: the woman or the therapist? Neither. First, there was a vulnerable child who experienced traumatic loss. My life is rich with experience: some of my choosing, some not. I no longer identify experiences as good or bad. Some are more challenging than others, yes, and it is our responses to these experiences that position us as victims. Mistakes are rich with learning if we let go of the blaming and shaming that is often our default. It is possible to outgrow the circumstances thrust unfairly upon us and surrender the faulty belief that good lives are doled out as rewards to the "chosen ones".

I have had many, many experiences, but I now know that none of them set my value as a human being unless I choose it. What causes the "good" or "bad" outcomes for me as a person is my response. My reactions, actions, and subsequent choices as a response to the experience is what will create negative or positive outcomes for me.

Some decades ago, I was finally able to reach a place of gratitude for life experiences I felt were unfair as a younger woman. I felt singled out by the universe, convinced I had an "Excrement Here" sign hanging over my head. I am now in a place where I can recognise that the growth I achieved by getting to the other side of those experiences has set me free. The more intense and painful the memories, the higher my gratitude. Yes, it was a process; first I had to grieve, let go of my story of how things should have been, let go of the "Why me?" story and move into acceptance.

Moving into acceptance created personal freedom and comfortableness in my skin I had not imagined possible and that is my genuine wish for you. First, we grieve as we connect the dots and realise our choices in the present moment were connected to the pain in our past. Then we move onto resolution, which is found in making a new agreement with our adult selves so that we can break out of the dysfunctional pattern. Integration is the final stage as we create boundaries, insist that others honour them and stop tolerating them when they purposely hurt us. Our self-esteem blossoms as we see how we can grow from our mistakes and update our core beliefs using an adult understanding.

I stand before you an unapologetic work in progress, which now excites me rather than filling me with shame. I no longer strive for or look for perfection in myself or others. I am a human renovation show; I constant check the plans, refining and improving, but I don't have a deadline or need to deal with difficult contractors because I am focused on enjoying the journey. I've got this!

I am convinced that every experience contains a gift. Admittedly, the wrapping will make us seriously question that premise at times, but I still believe it to be true. With gratitude comes power, and with acceptance comes even more power. If we adopt the attitude that any uncomfortable/challenging/stressful situation is not life punishing us, singling us out whilst the universe point its giant finger at us, screaming so all the world can hear that we are unlovable, imperfect, broken—whatever you have been telling yourself all these years—then we open up a menu of choices that we never knew existed.

I consider it part of my professional development to offer my clients a therapist who is prepared to work through the hard yards of becoming self-aware, never adopting the mindset that the job is done. It is also part of my personal development to offer the world an authentic, unapologetic version of myself and that can only happen by being honest. So here it is. My confession: *I have had personal experience of a dysfunctional relationship with hope. I too must remain vigilant to the triggers which could cause me to relapse.*

Thankfully, I became aware of my programming through taking on responsibility for the quality of my life and my relationships. Alarm bells now ring when I am at risk of repeating my old patterns. No matter how long it takes for the penny to drop, I permit myself to change direction. I am no longer in the business of being around people that don't value me, just because they carry the title of family, friend, lover, or colleague. I deserve better. I no longer wait for those to "get" me or permit me to be me. The only opinion that takes priority these days is my opinion of myself. I am the CEO of my experience and I am not seeking shareholders. I no longer take other people's bad behaviour personally. It flags they have work to do, just like we all do (if they want to that is). If they choose not to sort that stuff out, it is okay for me not to hang around.

We all have experienced different homes, families, generations, cultural and economic contexts; however, there are fundamentals constant to the human experience that help us thrive. We all need adequate food, safety, belonging, identity, health, and connection. We are wired to want to belong our very survival depends on it.

There was a time a long time ago in a faraway land that I did feel victimised by the circumstances of my life. I did struggle with the "Why me?" question; through self-reflection and self-acceptance, I was able to change that question to "Why not me?" As soon as I let go of blame, things began to change.

Blaming (picture an angry person pointing) is saying I am being controlled from outside of myself. Blame obscures our view of the choices we do have available to us. These choices don't have the power to change the past, but they can determine the quality of our here and now. We may not have control of the circumstances we are presented with but we can certainly choose if and how they will define us.

"Forces beyond your control can take away everything you possess except one thing, your freedom to choose how you will respond to the situation"
— Viktor E. Frankl

My father was killed in a workplace accident. He went to work in the morning and never came home. A family was changed forever before it had a chance to realise its potential. My developing brain responded in the only way it knew how, deciding that, somehow, if I was good enough, my father would come home. Our family would be complete again. Mum would stop crying and my younger brother would have the Daddy he desperately needed. I didn't manage to be good enough. I had no concept of how that would play out in my later life.

"The privilege of a lifetime is to become who you truly are"
— Carl Jung

Intentional or unintentional circumstances shape a child's' perception of the world due to the chemical reactions taking place in the brain. Stress and fear release cortisol, a hormone secreted by the adrenal glands. As we are now in a state of high alert, the neurotransmitter norepinephrine (a chemical that carries electrical impulse across our brain synapses) is released. All this happens in preparation to respond to perceived danger (whether it is real or not), snapping us into the present moment so that we can prepare to fight, flee, or freeze. Events that occurred in our past that were overwhelming, threatening, or abusive produce life-long somatic effects, such as the need for constant vigilance, anxiety, and depression. If you are reading this and still not sure whether it relates to you, I have put together a list that might help you answer that question.

Do any of these seem familiar?
- Abandonment issues
- High anxiety
- Denial (you will finish this and still think you had the perfect childhood)
- You carry feelings, desires, and secrets of other family members
- You have felt different, lonely and isolated most of your life
- You worry a lot, staying in your head to avoid feelings
- You are a control freak and you call it being helpful
- You feel inadequate and you hide within an addiction or your personality
- (being controlling, blaming, critical, perfectionist, wanting power and quick to anger).
- You have no personal boundaries
- It's all or nothing

- You go from zero to a hundred, whether the situation calls for it or not
- You keep repeating patterns that you consciously want to stop
- No matter where you begin or what you promise yourself, your life always end up in the same place
- You are not connected to your feelings, are unable to express them and don't know what you are supposed to be feeling
- You look like an adult but feel childlike and needy
- You can't recall painful events in your childhood
- You can't connect with your body and feelings
- You are still working to gain your parents' approval
- You are a rescuer
- You hold the secrets of your family or origin as well as your own
- You have difficulty communicating
- You are withdrawn, allowing yourself little excitement or fun
- You never feel satisfied
- You have been or are now in compulsive addictive behaviour
- You are still playing the same role in your family system
- You have intimacy problems
- You were abused as a child
- You have difficulty problem solving
- Your self-worth depends on your partners' or children's success/failure.
- You feel hollow if you are not in a relationship

- You are measured, judgemental and a perfectionist
- You have trouble trusting
- You take more than half of the responsibility, guilt or blame for what happens in your relationships
- You catastrophise and exaggerate
- You try to control your emotions and then have dramatic outbursts

Perspective

"There are three sides to every story: your side, my side, and the truth. And no one is lying. Memories shared serve each differently"

— Robert Evans

THE MUCH-AWAITED DAY FINALLY ARRIVES; despite all the things that could (and did) go wrong, we have managed to reach adulthood. Happy Dance! Now that we are armed with the superpowers that come with being an adult, we can finally see things as they are and check out those core beliefs formed in our childhood. You get to be the master of your destiny but you will need to connect with your inner detective first. Be prepared—there will be surprising and unexpected experiences.

It is also important to point out that you will only see what you are ready to see. This self-awareness and personal growth can be quick or slow, depending on the individual. We need to move at the pace that is right for us and sometimes we might need some help from our friendly neighbourhood therapist. Warning: avoid the trap of comparing yourself with how you think somebody else is doing. As some wise person once said, there is no competition in your life's journey.

"The tip of the neighbour's iceberg often looks very nice"
— Roy A. Ngansop

When we look back on our childhoods with fresh grown-up eyes and see what was there the whole time, it is not unusual to be stunned at first, followed by a gamut of emotions. It is very easy to become a vigilante at this point in the process. You could find yourself starting to plot and plan your revenge for the perceived injustices and wrongs committed against you. DO NOT GO THERE. You are at the very beginning of the journey and you have yet to climb down from the tip of the iceberg. Your job is to do nothing but be present and wait till you have the full picture. Blaming and finger-pointing need to be resisted; they serve no purpose and will only distract you from the task at hand. This is the time where you need to slow down and look at the situation from your newly-empowered adult perspective.

"To grow up is to stop putting blame on parents"
— Maya Angelou

I will pause for a moment to clarify that there is a big difference between blame and accountability. When we blame, we are saying "things are not working for me but it's not my fault". Accountability is much different because we acknowledge where the responsibility lies and hold the party accountable for the behaviour.

As we know, your core beliefs were formed by your child self. You were doing the best you could with a brain that told you that you were the central character, responsible for everything happening around you. If you think that I might be trying to hide behind some brain development mumbo jumbo, just take a moment to look at it simply. And by simply, I mean REALLY simply.

Have you ever seen how a toddler responds when asked to hide or play a game of peek-a-boo? They are way too cute as they giggle with delight at how clever they are at hiding. After placing their hands over their eyes, they are convinced you can't see them. Even with this limited perspective, the toddler is forming core beliefs.

All that happens in the world is a direct reaction to everything that we think, feel, or do: "Mum and Dad are fighting because I forgot to put out the rubbish", "my brother is sad because I ate the last chip", "I am a bad person because our family pet died". Whether it is praise or punishment that is being handed out, all roads lead to you.

Even our teenage self is convinced that all eyes are on us; we feel judged, scrutinised, visible. "I'm fat", "I'm ugly", "I'm stupid" —the list goes on. You are still forming and reinforcing core beliefs at this stage of development.

Growing up is hard. Our brains and bodies are doing their best to realise their potential and keep healthy. Just to make it even more of a challenge, why don't we throw some more complications into the mix? Remember our list of maybes? We are left to make sense of these "maybes" the best way we can with the limited capacity available to us.

This is why it is possible to have multiple siblings in a family who have very different opinions of what it was like to have grown up in that family. Each sibling may have different core beliefs that shaped their personality. Nobody has got it wrong; it is all about our perspective, determined by our stage of brain development, which in turn determined how we process the "maybes" when they happened. That perspective is also determined by things such as birth order, the stage of brain development (age), and how our caregivers responded specifically to us.

When we open up to the possibility of other outlooks, we move from the restrictive black and white world of a child into the multi-dimensioned world of adulthood. It is possible to comprehend that rejections of our perspective are not a rejection of us; they are simply a different point of view. That point of view can exist without being a threat to us. All we need to do is respect the other parties' right to have a different opinion. We can disagree with each other and still maintain a safe space and personal connection.

This is counter-intuitive for many of us because our families of origin demanded otherwise. To be different, to think differently or to hold a different opinion was seen as an act of treason against the family unit. Not sure if this applied to your family? Take a moment to think about the discussions that took place around the family dinner table regarding politics, religion, sports and customs; they are the obvious topics that highlight very quickly if different perspectives are tolerated. You will have members of the family who vote a certain way, eat a certain way or live in certain areas and have no idea why, other than "that is what our family does". There will be no recollection of a directive; however, it is understood that stepping outside the family norm will result in negative consequences. There are rules regarding how we are meant to operate in these types of families:

- **Control**: You must be in control of your feelings, behaviour, and relationships.
- **Perfectionism:** You must be right about everything.
- **Mythmaking**: What problem? There isn't a problem. Understood?
- **Incompletion**: Stay upset and confused—forget resolving differences.
- **Unreliability**: Don't trust anyone and you won't be disappointed.
- **Denial of the five freedoms** (feelings, thoughts, perceptions, wants, and imaginings)
- **No talking honestly**

It is from these rules we will develop the values that we carry into adulthood because they are consistent with the values of our family and guarantee membership. We get to belong.

Comparison

SOCIAL MEDIA IS NOT THE place to make new friends if you have a core belief or relationship template that hasn't worked for you in face to face relationships. If you have a history of hurt and enough optimism still burning within you that the "one" is out there, you are vulnerable to the not so pure among us who are waiting for people just like you. Often when we have been hurt badly, we retreat to online platforms for connection because it seems easier, safer and provides a bit of distance to protect ourselves.

The flaw in this rationale is that the opportunities to deceive, manipulate, bully, and abuse actually *increase* on such platforms. It is considerably easier for people with less than pure intentions to take advantage of those walking this earth with core beliefs that have us convinced we are not able to link into a healthy, supportive, respectful relationship. If we have not healed that core belief before we venture out onto social media, we are setting ourselves up for a world of pain.

Human beings connect through communication and the greater proportion of that communication is conveyed through our bodies. The person in front of us may have words a million flowing out of their mouths but it will be their bodies and the way they occupy the space will tell us the most about them. We lose access to that in online forums. If we have the propensity to misread the intentions of the people standing directly in front of us, we will have minimal hope of getting it right when the person is hidden behind a computer screen. The truth is, just like you, everybody else on the planet can be whoever they want to be in this environment.

It goes much deeper than filters and Snapchat bunny ears. Some deceptions will be unintentional and that creates problems in and of itself; others are intentionally out to deceive. Photos are edited, blemishes removed, bodies enhanced and personas created. Vulnerability is increased tenfold because, in our efforts to protect ourselves, we have unconsciously chosen to distance ourselves from who we are and created someone we believe will be rewarded with likes, shares and followers. If you are not solid in who you are and actively seek validation from strangers, you are playing with fire.

I am not saying that your modifications are intended to harm others. What I am pointing out is because you hold unconscious core beliefs about your value that are not positive, it can harm you. When you are editing yourself for acceptance by others, you are reinforcing the unconscious belief that you are not good enough. You are behaving this way because you are seeking genuine connection and you believe that the unedited version of yourself will not help you get there.

You also need to remember that you are not the only person who can use editing. Dishonest people deliberately create personas to exploit the naive and vulnerable. Their sole motivation is to exploit those of us who are desperate for connection, to belong, to demonstrate to our families/friends/colleagues that our lives are just as shiny as what they are sharing. What we forget to consider is that they too could be creating an online fantasy.

Comparison is cancer, resulting in distress, depression, despair, and death. Super gloomy, I know, but in far too many situations this is the reality of being online. Again, I repeat, if you are not solid in who you are, you will fall into the trap of comparing your life with fantasy-filled (and incredibly inaccurate) representations on social media.

These platforms can be particularly dangerous for those of us who are predisposed to toxic hope. We are quick to fill in the gaps with our hope-fuelled imaginations in the same way that we fill in the gaps for the people who let us down in our daily lives. Online, it is even easier to imagine ourselves in the spaces that exist within this one-dimensional communication.

Am I anti-social media? What I am is pro getting your relationship with hope sorted out before you convince yourself that being behind a computer screen is the best way to connect. The odds are not in your favour and you may connect with individuals who are only seeking what you can do for them.

Hope is Not a Strategy

"To suffer unnecessarily is masochistic rather than heroic"
— Viktor E. Frankl

MANY HAVE DEVELOPED AN OVER-RELI-ANCE on hope and have overlooked the need for goals and *timeframes* (note the emphasis here, people), not only for accountability but to flag the time to update the plan. If there is to be any chance of success with any course of action we decide to take, we need to REVIEW – ASSESS – REFINE constantly. Hoping for ten years that someone is going to finally stop treating you like a doormat is an example of not having a timeframe.

If you are caught in a constant cycle—repeating the same behaviours and arriving at the same destination that makes you feel bad about yourself and the world in general—you need to review your game plan. Tweak it, change it, abandon it—whatever you need to do. Goals are achieved when they are realistic and your actions are congruent with your thinking. The degree of difficulty intensifies when these goals relate to relationships.

This is because the goal is shared and its success is reliant on all parties being equally invested. Further still, this will only be possible if these relationships provide safe opportunities for open, honest dialogue and all parties have a clear understanding of what the desired outcome is. If you are the sole creator of the group goal and are the only one who knows what you are trying to achieve, that is not a goal. It is not hope either. It is a dream that, over time, will become a nightmare.

Confused? Let me put it this way: your goal is to climb over a brick wall. Your first course of action might be to run towards it, take a big leap, and hopefully find yourself on the other side. If your hopeful course of action leads you to slam face-first into the brick wall, you would be stunned, surprised and more than a little disappointed—not to mention the throbbing pain where your cranium made contact with the wall.

Here lies your challenge. The wall is still there and you are still on the wrong side of it. You still have not seen what is on the other side and you are no quitter. The next logical course of action would be to review your plan, create a Plan B or abort the plan altogether. After careful consideration, you may wonder if your inability to leap over the wall was more bad luck than lack of capability and decide to try one more time. If you are successful, great—time to celebrate! If not, you might decide to abandon your goal or go next door and borrow a ladder.

Now, let's address the elephant in the room. The one possible option that no one in their right mind would consider, where you choose to repeatedly run at the wall until you are concussed and confused. Bloodied, bruised, and baffled because, despite your best efforts, you are still on the wrong side of the wall! Am I sounding a little on the crazy side here?

Good! It *should* sound crazy. Such a suggestion is ludicrous. No one would consciously choose to do that to themselves. Yet for some of us, this is our reality in certain emotionally-loaded areas of our lives: relationships with our partner, family, friends, colleagues, even ourselves. We keep throwing ourselves into the same brick wall, knocking ourselves senseless while hoping this time will be different. This is then followed by a genuine surprise that we have had such a result.

False hope is *not* about not taking any action. False hope, the hope that leads to self-harm, causes us to repeat destructive actions over and over again by convincing us that we will get a different result. False hope, like any addiction, can find us locked into repeating that action for decades whilst we remain oblivious to the enormous personal price that has been paid.

"Most of us are imprisoned by something. We're living in darkness until something flips on the switch"
— Wynonna Judd

I'm disappointed that I have not been able to find a definitive attribution for the quote that changed my life. Two thousand and seventeen was the year the long-overdue metaphorical bucket of water was emptied on my head. I had spent a lifetime soul searching, crying rivers, trying to make sense of where I was going wrong and why I still didn't feel happy with who I was. I read a truckload of self-help books, attended hours of training and seminars, watched inspirational movies, and studied when finally... BOOM! With these five little words, the penny dropped.

My cage door was blown off the hinges! Everything became crystal clear. I could see the deceit I had used to protect myself from the truth of some of the relationships (by this time, I was down to the shortlist) that I was struggling with. I was free to let it go. All that was left was for me to walk through that open door.

"Hope is not a strategy."

I know I keep repeating it, but I seriously love, love, love this. Personally, it feels like a Dr. Martin Luther King "Free at Last!" kind of moment.

I am not ashamed to admit that I like a good story; at times, I have been guilty of gilding the lily. Hand on my heart, this is not one of those times. The shift was seismic and the relief instant as a lifetime of burden metaphorically slid from my shoulders. I lifted my head from the book and scanned the room, half expecting the walls of my house to have been reduced to rubble just as my core belief had been. I admit to feeling panic at first. I was overwhelmed at the magnitude of my realisation. I tried closing the book, closing my eyes, closing my mind to return those words to the status of "unseen", but I couldn't. I would never be the same again. I suddenly felt exposed by the truth that, up until this point, I hadn't been able to see.

There it was. The truth behind my protective layers. I was balancing on the cusp of great change and it felt more like a precipice. Was I scared? Hell yes! Strangely, I also felt a lightness. Optimism. I was excited! I now knew the why and needed to move to the how. How would this insight translate into improvements to the way I had habitually related to people in my life? In trying to solve this puzzle, I was surprised to find a complex web of actions, reactions and reframing I had created to protect me from the truth of my dysfunctional relationships.

"Hope is not a strategy."

No more avoidance. It was time to put my underpants over my trousers and tie a tea towel around my neck like the superhero I now felt like and get on with it. I had work to do!

Fact: dogged dedication to hope had not led me to happiness. The door of the cage was swinging wide open; all I had to do was walk through it. Hope had been a go-to position with toxic people for so long that I failed to notice when, as a protection strategy, it had started to smell.

It was a surprise to discover the extent to which I had fragmented myself to stay connected to people who should have loved me but didn't or couldn't do so in a safe way. Similar to a dropped mirror, there were pieces of me scattered everywhere. Yes, at first I was overwhelmed by the size of the job before me. A quick tip: people will say they love you and say they're sorry, but if their love hurts you and their apology doesn't change their behaviour, you are not being loved. You are being controlled by your need to be loved.

Back to putting myself back together, which involved collecting all of the shattered shards of self so that I could once again become whole. Like all good dramas, I had a backing track playing constantly, unnoticed in the background of my life: classic Hope hits like "if only", "one more chance", "next time will be different", "I'll try harder" and the chart-topping "I know they love me".

Hoping is a bit like wishing: nice to do, but the conversion rate to miracles is a little on the low side. Let's not get side-tracked; I am not denying the existence of miracles. I am just being frank. To move from hoping to an outcome requires some elbow grease on your part. My hoping regarding certain people was never going to end well. All I had was a pocket full of good intentions, high tolerance to abuse, and a subconscious packed with outdated core beliefs. There was nothing I couldn't forgive or make an excuse for, no matter how deeply I had been wounded. I tolerated behaviours I would never have accepted in any other sphere of my life.

It was time. I now knew beyond a shadow of a doubt that my hope had been misspent, gone beyond the realms of reasonable-ness, and could never have achieved the outcome I was seeking.

Love

"Don't rush into something until you're sure it actually exists"
— Susan Gale

THROUGH NO FAULT OF OUR own, many of us don't understand what real love looks and feels like. Society loves to throw the word around to explain our relationship to all sorts of situations, possessions, and the like; quite frankly, the word "love", just like "hope", has fallen victim to overuse. How many times have you heard someone say "I love my car", "I love my iPhone", "I love ice cream", "I love the great outdoors", "I love ..." (feel free to populate with as many things you can think of)?

Love has been used as a tool to sell products that will "complete" us. Looking for love is the subject for reality shows who put people hoping to find the real thing in all sorts of artificial situations subject to public scrutiny. Love has been cheapened, reduced to a concept, entertainment for the masses: a panacea light-years from the truth.

The word "love" on its own is just a word. For it to be powerful and relevant, it needs to be supported by the actions congruent with love. It is also important to recognise that expectations of love are not universal because we will all have different working definitions of what it is and does, formed from our subjective experience. We form this definition of love as children and then seek it from our adult relationships. Often what is offered is only half of the boxed set, leaving the objects of this love hurt and confused. This confusion experienced, especially in childhood, leads to a difficulty in identifying the real deal when we become adults. This is why so many of us end up in adult relationships that are abusive in varying scales.

So when we have been misinformed or become confused about love, our challenge as adults (should we choose to accept it) is to learn what real love is. Often, our definition of love is simplistically focused on sex. We equate being desired by others as the key to fulfillment. This is not at all surprising; we are bombarded with mixed messages about love from an early age from our families, the institutions we come in contact with, the media, and the wider world.

"Love" songs bruising the radio waves saturate our brains with words we don't understand from the time we are in our mother's womb. Lyrics such as "you complete me" are misleading and often lead to a world of pain. This so-called romantic lyric suggests we have come into this world with part of us missing, destined to endlessly roam the Earth searching for the elusive missing piece. For many of us, they will be playing our song because of the core beliefs we hold about ourselves.

We are in love with love. In our quest to feel loved, we will doggedly pursue becoming whole, convincing ourselves that this one is *the one*; if it fails, we will continue seeking for as long as it takes. Our failure to be a complete person is our badge of shame, obvious to everyone that meets us. Holding this knowledge as truth, we believe the world sees us as dysfunctional and unlovable and will continue to do so until the magic moment when, just like an IKEA flat pack, we are put together by the one who loves us.

It is no wonder with an instruction sheet full of as many mistakes and assumptions as this we find ourselves put together with at least one or two screws missing—in some cases, entire sections! Not unlike that much-anticipated bookcase for the study that, when put together, looks nothing like the picture or has a disturbing lean to it. Our newfound love, our salvation from skirting on the perimeter of wholeness, may look—and even feel—like a relationship, but after you start loading up the shelves, things start to get wobbly. You realise that, just like your flat pack bookcase, it is not going to hold up for the purpose you had intended.

There is another part of the "comprehensive" (yes, this is me being sarcastic) definition of love that we must first embrace before we decide to tumble between the sheets, oohing and aahing and convincing ourselves that we are now complete. Our judgement goes out the window when confronted with the heady combination of hormones and being in love with the idea of love. It is during this out of body phase that we convince ourselves of all sorts of aberrations: confusing possessiveness with protectiveness, rudeness with sensitivity, aggressiveness for assertiveness, sarcasm for humour—the list goes on and on. We do this because our "incomplete" selves tell us that they are small prices to pay to achieve completeness. We want the public humiliation of being incomplete to stop, so we are willing to pay the price. After all, anything worth having is worth working for—right? Even if you are the one doing all the work.

It is not uncommon to find ourselves fumbling around in the dark tolerating touches that are uncomfortable, predicting what the other person needs or wants based on some highly-edited Hollywood version of love. In our efforts to complete ourselves, we find ourselves role-playing between the sheets, searching for intimacy and connection.

The sad irony is that on our quest for love, we will get naked with a virtual stranger but not be able to speak our truth. We try to hide our truth because we know that we are not enough and must do our best to make sure they don't find out how broken we are. We will find it impossible to ask for our needs to be met. Our cliché response when (and if) we are asked what we want will be something like "I don't know—what do you want?", "I don't mind", or "You choose". This is all is code for "I don't matter and my needs are unimportant and if my new love doesn't realise that they are mistaken and a car crash is inevitable".

Is it any wonder we fail at relationships? It is not our unlovability standing between us and the relationships that we want—it's us! How can we find that person who loves us unconditionally when we are not prepared to love ourselves in the same way? What sort of message are we sending out into the world? "Please love me because I find myself so flawed, so repugnant, that I couldn't possibly do it myself." We are so desperate to not spend any more time with ourselves that we rush into relationships, seeing what we want to see. When things settle, we discover we have found the same arse that we are always attracted to, just dressed differently.

We need to stop being in love with love. It is not a way to escape yourself or your history. It is something that comes to us when we have done the work on ourselves and we are besotted with our own company. We will find the real deal when we don't need it.

Loving You

"Sugarcoating things makes people feel better, but it also gives them false hope, and it keeps them holding onto the wrong people"
— **Sonya Parker**

F WE ARE SINCERE IN our quest to find true love then we must first fall in love with ourselves. This, you may have noticed, is light-years away from experiences such as getting undressed in the dark, wearing makeup to bed, breathing in every time your loved one looks at you, denying that you have ever passed wind or grown hair on your toes, and consenting to things that make you feel uncomfortable at the least and dirty at the worst.

We need to fall in love with our entire self: the parts we are proud of, the parts we are ambivalent about and the parts we are ashamed of. When we can offer and accept this unconditional love from ourselves, we can then find true love with others. We won't be caught up in the destructive cycle of trying to "earn" love. If we seek love with and from others without achieving this, we are operating from shame. If we feel we need to act in a certain way to be lovable, "compensate" for our shortcomings, or bury the parts of us that are "unworthy of love", we are seeking love for the wrong reasons.

When we believe that we are unworthy of love, our relationships will mirror this belief back to us. This is due to the fabrications that we offer in our pursuit of a relationship that will attract the very things we don't need. We offer what we believe others need to see, hear, and experience to love us. This is shame-based behaviour born from shame-based thinking, which leads to shame-based acting. If we believe that we are broken and that the only way to be in a relationship is to plaster over our perceived cracks, we become disconnected from who we are. You may have heard the term "authentic self" thrown around and, when caught up in the shame cycle, the term will have confused you.

The natural consequence of our behaviour is to experience devastation when others can't tell who we are and meet our needs. What we don't, won't, or can't acknowledge is that buried beneath our compensating behaviours lies the motivation for them : shame, pulsing its poison through our reality. Shame will encourage us to bury our true selves so deeply that we will eventually become unrecognisable to ourselves.

Lost to ourselves, we hope to discover the way back through the eyes of others. There lies the paradox. We have buried who we are to earn love, unaware that our loved ones can only reflect the façade that we have presented to them. This person is unrecognisable to us. It angers us because our loved ones don't know who we are; they appear to be blind to what we have not shown them. We are disappointed by their lack of super-powers and then turn their inability to provide our self-worth as confirmation of how flawed we are. Not for a moment do we question the impossibility of the challenge we have set them. Nor do we question why we are so committed to such self-destructive, soul-destroying behaviour.

How could they see what you have not revealed? It is not reasonable to expect this from another person, as their experience of you is defined by what you have disclosed about yourself. Such an unrealistic expectation sets you up for a fall because all you have ever shown them is a highly-edited, sanitised version. We are blissfully ignorant of the cost of each revision, each failed relationship, each disappointment, each "I'll try harder next time": the growing distance between the reality of your pure self and the construction you have used to gain approval. There is no trail of breadcrumbs leading us back to ourselves; we held so little respect for the real us that we destroyed the path.

We are well-rehearsed magicians, creating an illusion that the targets of our affection find entertaining at first. The downside of the illusion is that it is not sustainable as it is destined to end the way of all magic shows. To be successful, magic needs to be brief, meteoric; an amazing moment in time. If the audience is exposed to the magic for too long, believability wanes and questions bubble predictably to the surface of our conscious minds. The magic is lost and it is seen for what it is: an illusion, a manipulation of reality. We start to notice the cracks and inconsistencies.

Magic is possible in relationships. Magical, love-filled, durable relationships are created with honesty, not illusion; transparency, not secrecy; connection, not sleight of hand; self-acceptance, not a rejection of self; genuine curiosity, not judgement;

being present, not hiding amongst magical puffs of smoke. We will grow to resent the object of our desire for not being able to see what we have artfully hidden from ourselves.

We demand in our passive ways proof that we are love-able, that we are wanted. We set our loved ones up to fail. We have handed them a poisoned chalice. If they do love us, they can only love what we have been prepared to show them. Ultimately, this leads to us feeling let down and we internalise their failure as validation of our story of shame. Hurt, disappointed, bemused, confused and shamed, we do what we always do—we withdraw. We draw our cards even closer to our chest, convinced that we need to go even further underground. If only someone had told us that all we had to do was be ourselves, flaws and all.

Other lies about love that do as much damage as "you complete me" include (but are not confined to) such gems as:

- Once you move in together, get married and have a child, you will be happy
- Love conquers all
- The person of your love will just "get" you
- Love just happens; it is unexpected and incredibly romantic
- Love means never having to say you're sorry
- You can change someone if you try hard enough
- Looks determine the quality of the catch
- Sometimes you have to settle; all the good ones are taken

- If you have had a failed relationship, you have missed the relationship boat
- You have to hit rock bottom and then be rescued
- Love at first sight is everyone's experience
- Your life is on hold until you find *the one*
- Your happiness will just happen when you fall in love
- There is no conflict
- They will change
- Happy ever after

Pain Goes Away

"People will do anything, no matter how absurd, to avoid facing their own souls"

— Carl Jung

THE KEY TO STOPPING THIS insanity lies within awareness, honesty, and the willingness to get uncomfortable. I know that you are probably thinking that it is not that bad or that, eventually, it will change. Here are some behaviours which, when out of balance, can suggest that you are spending your hope in ways that are limiting your potential at best and harmful and destructive at worst:

- You are the master compromiser, apology maker, speed forgiver and peacemaker in your family.
- You feel compelled to do the "right thing" for others, even if it conflicts with your plans or your efforts are repeatedly and predictably unappreciated, criticised, or discounted.
- You will put your plans on hold until you have fulfilled your commitment to your family.

- You have a list of "shoulds" relating to your family. Thinking of these or the consequences of not fulfilling them fills you with guilt and dread.

- You often feel hurt, angry, and disappointed in your family but are unable to express how you feel to them.

- The mere thought of being hurt, angry, or disappointed fills you with guilt.

- You go the extra mile constantly. You volunteer and say you have the capacity to do things, even though you know you will have to stay up for most of the night to achieve it.

- You don't feel able to ask your family or friends to help you because you feel that it is too much to ask. You don't want to be a burden.

- You are the "go-to" person in the family. The family member who always has time and never says no.

- Every personal relationship in your life has involved you "rescuing" the other party in some way. This applies equally to work, friendship, and romantic relationships. You rely heavily on forgiveness and availability to make these relationships work.

- If you were to ask for something in return, you would be disappointed and hurt to find that you receive nothing.

- When you do break free from these relationships, you promise yourself "never again" and are stunned when you inevitably choose the exact same personality type, unaware that you have deceived yourself by choosing to see what you wanted to see in the other person.

- Rather than admitting this to yourself, you find yourself defending these relationships to friends and strangers alike, genuinely surprised that they can't see what you can see in this person. Your response to their well-meaning feedback will look something like this: "But you don't know them as I do", "But you need to understand they have had a terrible life", "But they were only joking—you don't get their sense of humour as I do", "But this is only till they get a job, get better, get their inheritance... "
- The only holidays you take are to help others (looking after your friends' children, caring for friends or family recovering from surgery, house sitting while others go on holidays, etc.).
- Your conversations tend to be all about the person you are spending time with
- When asked your opinion, you will respond with "I don't know—what do you think?"
- When asked to choose a movie, restaurant, etc., you will always respond with "I don't mind. You choose".
- You worry constantly about what other people think of you; if someone is offended, you immediately think you are to blame.
- The worst thing in the world is for people to think that you are selfish.

- Choosing anything for yourself feels selfish.
- You apologise constantly. You open conversations with "I'm sorry" and when people offer feedback of any kind, your response is always "Sorry".
- You don't have valuable opinions; everyone else's are far more important.
- When asked what you want, need or think, you are genuinely stumped for an answer.
- Humour and vagueness are some of the strategies you use to deflect to a safer topic (AKA anyone else in the room).
- No matter the location—the office, a friend's place or your own home—you are always predicting others' needs. You find yourself doing lovely things for people that you would love to receive yourself.
- You never operate the television remote when someone else is in the room. You defer to others on channel selection.
- You are always clearing up after others. Parties are a particular favourite; you can be found in the kitchen washing dishes or serving food and insist on leaving the host's house cleaner then you found it. When told not to worry, your automatic response is "I don't mind" (shorthand for "Please see me as being worthy of having in your life").
- When you host a party, you don't allow anyone to help. You claim that you will get it done tomorrow. People leave and you stay up until the small hours

returning your home to cleanliness because you can't stand waking up to the mess in the morning.

· You find it difficult, if not impossible, to ask for your needs to be met. If you do overcome your fear and ask, you are immediately ashamed of yourself. You retract your request the instant it comes out of your mouth, explaining away your truth, apologising and compensating for being an imposition.

· You compare yourself to others, wishing you were like them (but you are not smart enough, pretty enough, or lucky). It doesn't occur to you that you are equal to them.

· You are constantly compensating for not being enough.

· Any compliment offered cannot be received and are returned with a list of your deficits and faults.

· People label you with names such as "emotional", "needy", "different".

Phew! That was one long list and I am sure I have missed some (or many). Whether you engage in one or all of these behaviours, each is an opportunity—no, an *invitation*—to stop. Your self-worth depends upon it.

It feels so unfair that, no matter what efforts you go to, nothing changes. You don't feel accepted or respected. There is a very good reason for this: your lack of personal boundaries has led to you being taken for granted. Your actions lead people to assume that your life is not that full, your work not that important, and that your own family is so dysfunctional that any time away from them is a blessing. Everyone is doing you a favour by distracting you from your tedious and boring existence.

Acceptance

"There is something truly restorative, finally comforting, in coming to the end of an illusion—a false hope"
— Sue Miller

F WE BREAK IT DOWN even further, hope is based on dissatisfaction with the present. We are dreaming of or desiring our lives to be better or different somehow. If we are caught up in hoping or are acting in ways to influence a different reality, then our current one is being controlled by our wanting.

We are wanting to be over there instead of here, to be thinner, prettier. We are wanting a happy family, a great love life, children... and the list goes on. What this says is that the reality we have is not as good as what is going on in everybody else's life. We want to be anywhere else.

It is resisting the truth of your "here", the creator of all the pain and suffering and self-flagellation in your life. Our family may be dysfunctional and abusive, our relationship with ourself light-years away from being healthy and loving, our romantic relationships fleeting and unsatisfactory or non-existent, our parenting skills far from our intentions, but wanting it to be different doesn't change anything. We keep hoping that by being the best doormat ever that, somehow, our here and now will change. We hope until our hearts break. We fall into our beds and we start the madness all over again.

In my view, this is a form of self-harm (unconscious, yes, but harm just the same), justified because it has a noble name and we back it up with noble actions. The truth of the matter is that it is not so noble because we have forgotten ourselves, disconnected from ourselves—we no longer know or even like ourselves. Our dishonesty disgusts us and we punish ourselves by relentlessly chasing the missing parts of ourselves.

The truth is there is a way back to wholeness. Peace and happiness are possible and it is not through false hope. The path is one of acceptance. Yes, acceptance. Take off the blinkers, get rid of all the deception, fabrication, justification, and see the current situation for what it truly is. Understand that the pain you fear will be nowhere as harmful to you as the pain you have experienced for decades. Examine in the light for the first time every single, ugly detail of the situation—not to beat yourself up, assign blame, take revenge or tell the world how bad you have had it. Accept the situation and set the intention to create a better one. We need to get one thing straight: acceptance is not the same as resignation. Acceptance is not the same as surrendering.

Up until this point, you have responded to the world without even thinking about the motivations for your actions. You have certain situations that trigger automatic responses. These responses often take you by surprise, lead to negative outcomes, or simply don't work. They don't add value to the quality of your life. When we move from living unconsciously, feeling victimised by our circumstances and embedded in repeating self-destructive behaviours, to acceptance, the whole world opens up.

Acceptance puts you in the driver's seat. You recognise what is present, consciously choose the thoughts about the situation/s and commit to moving forward, rather than spinning your wheels in the muck and mud of your past. Addiction of any kind leads to the erosion of self-respect, self-worth, and the decimation of all relationships. The worst casualty is the relationship with the self. If we can't trust ourselves to call time on a situation, to exercise self-preservation, who can we trust?

> *"Every form of addiction is bad, no matter whether the narcotic be alcohol or morphine or idealism."*
> **— Carl Jung**

How can we know it is a hopeless situation? Simple: that situation no longer exists. It is a fragment of the past that we have responded to and formed a core belief around as a means of protection. We attempted to put the world right, but that world no longer exists. The people that had a part to play have changed, left, or lost interest in that particular piece of history. Some of them would have been ignorant of the impact of the experience on us and can only recollect how it impacted them. Hopeless sounds harsh—I don't mean it to, but the reality is that this core belief is rendering you powerless in the here and now. Quite frankly, you have suffered enough!

We hoped that our situation would someday magically transform into the "ideal" we have held in our mind's eye our whole life. We compromised, negotiated, begged, blackmailed, bullied, sulked, cried, yelled, shouted, pleaded and used every tool at our disposal whilst repeating the same old self-destructive loop: cry... try... repeat.

We tried everything except the most important thing of all: surrender. We continue to hope that we can pull off a two-person job with only one person doing the work. We deny ourselves permission to let it go and finally begin to live a full life. We've avoided the only place we have any influence: now.

In life, whatever the pursuit, we will be called upon to assess our course of action, the appropriateness of our investment, and the merit of continuing or not continuing depending on the situation. Relationships—biological or otherwise—are no different. Despite our best intentions, our hopes, aspirations and dreams, we will arrive at the point where abandoning hope is psychologically healthier and physically safer than holding on to it. This is not an easy decision to make and it is certainly not easy to do. However, I will argue that if you are reading this, what you have been doing to bring your hopes to fruition has been no picnic. There is a real difference between giving of yourself and giving up yourself. I know that because you have been in the business of giving up yourself you will perceive the letting go of hope as a defeat, a failure on your behalf. This, like so many other things you have been telling yourself, is simply not true.

The truth for us all is that we are here for one purpose: to reach our full potential. To realise the authentic expression of who we are so we can contribute our best to our close relationships and the big wide world in general. This is not possible when we are trapped in a way of relating to the world based on an "I'm not good enough story".

No matter how the story got there—no matter the intentions of the people around you, or how many mistakes and bad choices you have made—it is never too late to accept, let go and realise personal freedom. You can create a new direction fuelled by self-determination and personal power. A new relationship with yourself based on love and respect. A new hope—one that is born to support you, not suppress you, as you head into a new beginning.

The future should never come at the expense of the present and the present should not be lived as a sacrifice to the past. The quality of your past only gets to determine the quality of the present if you buy into the misinformation and misinterpretations. The sad part is that the keys to our happiness and fulfilment have always been available to us. Yet we live our adult lives reacting to the messages we internalised as rules for living as children. As adults with awareness and acceptance, we can make positive choices that help us grow and realise the quality relationships we crave. The relationships may not be with the people that we have worked so hard to keep in our lives, or the dynamic may shift to one that doesn't cost you your mental and physical health.

"But I know, somehow, that only when it is dark enough can you see the stars"
—Martin Luther King Jr.

How to Recognise Abuse

I F WE HAVE BEEN EXPOSED to certain patterns of behaviour for most of our life, those behaviours will be accepted as natural and normal in our relationships. If those patterns of behaviour are abusive, we will not recognise them as such because they are the norm. This is what makes it so difficult to identify if you are in an abusive relationship. Especially if you have been exposed to abuse that is right at the top of the Richter scale, "minor" expressions of abuse in your relationships will seem not so bad.

As human beings, we have needs. To thrive, we need those needs to be met, meaning that our behaviours are often motivated by attaining these needs. Some of these behaviours won't be ones that are helpful for our personal growth. The areas are grouped as follows:

- Air, food, drink, shelter, clothing, warmth, sex, sleep.
- Protection from elements, security, order, law, stability, freedom from fear.
- Friendship, intimacy, trust, and acceptance, receiving and giving affection and love.
- Being part of a group (family, friends, work).
- Esteem for oneself (dignity, achievement, mastery, independence) and the desire for reputation or respect from others (e.g., status, prestige).
- Self-actualisation (realising personal potential, self-fulfilment, seeking personal growth and peak experiences).

The "how" we live our lives, as we know, is primarily formulated in childhood. Our legacy as adults is to scrutinise this with adult eyes, compare it to social norms and come up with a blueprint that is more suitable and conducive to our personal growth. This blueprint needs to facilitate autonomy, self-expression and self-determination as we realise an unapologetic expression of who we are.

When we are sitting smack bang in the middle of our subjective experience and we have not been exposed to the faults in our blueprints, we will often miss cues that we are not quite plugged into relationships that are working for us. We accept the ones we have as normal when they are far from that.

If a relationship in any realm of your life—family, lovers, friends, or colleagues—has some or all of the following elements, then it is time for a spring clean. Get the dust out of your eyes and see what is happening.

Abuse unfortunately comes in different guises; it can be mental, physical, sexual, verbal, emotional, or a mixture of some or all. I want to be very clear: abuse in whatever manifestation has no place in a relationship. Manipulation, either overt or covert, is abuse. My apologies for the straight talk, but I know that you have made so many excuses for this behaviour that you will want to defend your loved one.

Your love has altered your reality. It's time to come home. I am metaphorically standing on the front porch, yelling your name, ringing the dinner bell. So listen, look, and look again if your default reaction is to resist what I am saying. If the time you share is tinged with anxiety based on your uncertainty on how things are going to turn out, that is not a safe place to be.

Signs that you are overdue for a change in your relationship (aka RED FLAGS)

- Positive times are rare. You always feel down/not good enough or you haven't done enough after spending time together.
- You are left so stressed that it impacts your work or home life.
- You find yourself constantly defending or explaining yourself.
- All you talk about with your friends is the chaos in the relationship.
- You say things to your friends that you are not able to say to the family.

- You listen/look out for gossip so you can correct what is being said about you.
- Family members gang up on you. Because you are on the outside, you start to question if there is something wrong with you.
- The relationship is entirely about the other person with no input from them at all.
- Relationships are one-sided; you are never able to do enough.
- You are only invited when you serve a purpose such as borrowing money. Getting paid back is not likely to happen.
- You are on the receiving end of the silent treatment, blame-games or no-win arguments where it is always your fault.
- You must agree with everything or you are shown the door.
- Your gut is telling you to "stop putting up with this" but you find yourself making excuses.
- You try talking about the problem and the responses just get meaner.
- You are surrounded by irrational, cruel people who love to argue and never look at their contribution to the situation.
- When you raise how you feel, you are told "it is just part of being a family".
- You are the only one that wants or sees the need for change.

· You can't accept the truth of their behaviour so you hope/believe that one day, the light will go on and they will realise the pain they are causing and stop.

· You have tried everything and you constantly end up abused and exhausted.

· You don't like the treatment you receive but are frightened of being alone so you stay and hope.

We can be related to and in love with people who are, quite frankly, toxic. I have mentioned these traits several times already in different ways, but it is an important message to internalise, absorb if you will. Soak it up until it becomes as natural to you as your current practice of making excuses for those toxic people in your life.

It also may be difficult to see at first. That is the power of a habit; we are so enmeshed in our patterns we will feel threatened by this new reality. It is a perfectly natural self-protection mechanism but, at the same time, it is incredibly dangerous. That is why I am dogged in my persistence in delivering this message. *You don't know what you don't know.* There is no judgement here but the reality—your reality—is that if you are putting up with this treatment, you are not in a safe place. I need you to wake up so you can take action and choose a life that you deserve. This is not living. It is existing, or simply surviving. Nobody deserves this kind of treatment, no matter what rubbish you have been drip-fed by the toxic people in your life. Nobody can feel whole or thrive in such an environment.

Toxic People 101

Read it once, read it twice, read it as many times as it takes.

Control, control, and then some more control

Out of control people look for ways to control others. Their life isn't working for them they want to feel good about themselves so they have no trouble doing so at your expense.

No respect for your boundaries ever

The word boundaries are not in their vocabulary. They show no respect. If you are dealing with well-adjusted adults respect of boundaries comes naturally to them.

Take, take, take (and when you have nothing left they will try and take more)

They will take whatever you have and then demand more. The only need of any importance in a relationship is theirs.

Never wrong

They are always right even when they are not. They will never admit to making a mistake, making an error in judgement, or saying anything wrong. Forget an apology. They will never take responsibility for anything happening in their lives.

Talking = lying

Honesty is not in their vocabulary. The world is not on their side; they are always the victim, and take no ownership at all.

Abuse unfortunately comes in a variety of flavours. One of the hardest to identify when you are sitting in the middle of the experience is emotional abuse because it is a pattern that often unfolds over time. It sneaks up on you. It includes intimidation, humiliation, manipulation, and verbal aggression, which all chip away and eventually erode the other person's self-worth, identity and dignity. It is not surprising that being subjected to this kind of behaviour in all likelihood will lead to mental health consequences: anxiety, depression, suicidal thoughts or behaviours, and post-traumatic stress disorder. You will often hear those subjected to emotional abuse saying things like "at least they don't hit me". If you are saying this to yourself in your relationships, please know that emotional abuse is equally as dangerous and unacceptable as physical abuse. It is important that you find yourself some support—the sooner, the better.

Behaviours that are potentially emotionally abusive are very broad and include intimidation, manipulation, refusal to ever be pleased, blaming, shaming, name-calling, insults, put-downs, sarcasm, infantilisation, silent treatment, trivialising, triangulation, sabotage, gaslighting, scapegoating, blame-shifting, projection, ranking and comparing, arbitrary and unpredictable inconsistency, threatening harm and forced isolation. I say "potentially" because it depends on context. There are a lot of people out there who appreciate sarcasm as humour. Again, that is fine as long as the joke is shared and isn't malicious in motivation.

Even if you are the most observant person in the world, emotional abuse can be so insidious that you don't notice it. This makes it possible for it to fly under the radar as it slowly builds over months, years—even decades. In such instances, self-esteem is eroded and the ability to trust yourself is eroded to the point that there is a vague sense of something being wrong but no certainty as to what.

Signs of Emotional Abuse

- Dismiss your feelings by making comments such as, "I'm saying this for your good, "It's all in your mind", "You're being too sensitive" or "I'm only kidding".

- Undermine self-esteem by name-calling, humiliation, criticism, sarcasm, ridicule, or other demeaning behaviour.

- Control you by swearing, yelling, or making threats.

- Neglect you (forgetting promises or staying out all night without calling).

- Use tone of voice, facial expressions to intimidate you.

- Tell you where you can go, who you can see and not allowing you to use the credit cards or have money

- Uses sex as a form of punishment. May demand or withhold sex. You know it is not safe to say no to sex.

- Make cruel comments about appearance, weight, race, or ethnic background.

- Twist words, manipulate, confuse, or play other mind games.

Stuck

A S CHILDREN, WE BELIEVE THAT we can make the people in our lives happy or sad just by the things we say and do. We have already spent a great deal of time on the "why" of that, so I won't go there again. Adult love requires attention, acceptance, appreciation, affection, and allowing; the possibility of us being able to achieve those things in our adult relationships are depending on the beliefs that were formed by our child self. Our family experience forms the model on which we base our concept of love and we then seek adult relationships that match (or don't match) that model. Many of us walk through our childhood with the belief that it is a responsibility to make the people we love happy. I am going to explain why that's not such a great idea.

Feeling obligated to keep someone else happy causes more harm than good. The truth is you cannot be responsible for someone's mental outlook. It's impossible. You can provide a healthy and safe environment for other people to be happy in, yes. You can give other people a chance to be happy. But, ultimately, the choice to be happy is theirs. Someone else's happiness will never be your choice. It's outside of your control for several reasons.

Some people just don't want to be happy. Hard to believe, I know, but some people just love wallowing in their misery because they love the attention it gets them. This is a sign that someone is still operating from their child self. A dopamine release gives them the emotional high they are seeking through their behaviour, but it soon wears off so they will need you to rush in rescue them again; this time, they will create even more impressive circumstances to get your attention. Whatever you do, nothing is going to make this person happy. Your goal and theirs isn't a match.

You will not be able to make some people happy because they just don't like you. These people are happy in general, but not around you. This is a blessing in disguise—you do not need to doubt whether you should waste your time here. Don't chase them. There is a world full of people who will be happy to have you around them, so pick them. You deserve to be around people like that.

Happiness can be used to manipulate you. We have all had an experience of people that come on way too strong or try too hard; our instinct is to back off. It's okay. This is normal. When someone comes on too strong, our brains tell us to put up our guard. Resistance is a form of protection. Again, it's natural. Where the manipulation comes in is when someone senses that you want them to like you and they use it against you. They see your vulnerability and they string you along. They see your desire to make them happy and leverage it to manipulate you. All too often, the person you're chasing is keeping their happiness one step ahead of you on purpose.

Sometimes supporting someone is the worst thing you can do for them. Instead of helping them become stronger, you are unintentionally doing the opposite. Remember the butterfly? Tough love is tough not because it hurts the person on the receiving end, but because it hurts the person who is being tough. You can't live another person's life for them because it is not good for them and while you are holding them up, you are not living your own life.

You can't give someone happiness. Happiness is part of your health and, like the rest of your health, it can't be shared. You have to give people space to figure out how to be happy on their own. They need to learn to be happy without you. They need to learn to create their happiness from within.

When you pay attention only when someone is feeling sorry for themselves, you're training them to feel sorry for themselves. You're also training them to need you. This will come from our need to be lovable and not have anything to do with them at all. We martyr ourselves to earn love and approval. We offer them what we feel we missed out on. The way to add value is to live your life as an example of what can be achieved and, in the meantime, learn how to be happy without needing others to rely on you.

Life is short. You only get one and it is a waste to spend all of your time and energy trying to make other people happy. All you achieve is the emptying of your cup. Live your life, do what makes you happy and, through your actions, you will set an example of what's possible and provide inspiration to others so they can decide to create their own happy life (or not).

It is too big a job to be solely responsible for another person's happiness. The burden is far too great. Our reasons begin innocently enough: we care, and we want others to be happy. Ultimately, this is a path to anxiety.

- We believe the responsibility for others' happiness rests on our shoulders.
- We do everything we can think of to make sure others are happy.
- Others aren't always happy (that's just the way life is).
- We feel a sense of guilt when others aren't fully happy, as if we have failed them.
- We feel anxious because we've failed. We almost feel a sense of perfectionism about this; others must not only be happy, but be perfectly happy because we did our happiness job perfectly. This impossible standard increases our anxiety.
- Often, we believe that if we cater to what everyone wants, they'll be happy and we can avoid unpleasant conflict. Conflict increases anxiety but, ironically, trying hard to please others to avoid conflict causes greater anxiety.
- We worry about others, and we blame ourselves for their unhappiness. We come to fear the imagined consequences of this and increase our fear/worry

with an endless stream of "what ifs", which in turn causes more anxiety.

And so the cycle goes. Feeling solely responsible for the happiness of others, no matter how well-intended, causes anxiety. It also erodes our self-confidence, energy, and the opportunity to focus on creating our own happy lives. Happiness can't be achieved when we give up ourselves. There is a huge difference between the giving of oneself and giving up oneself. If your whole life is dedicated to realising happiness for others, there will never be time for you. That, my friend, breaks my heart.

Goodbye Toxic People

"The most important relationship we can all have is the one you have with yourself, the most important journey you can take is one of self-discovery. To know yourself, you must spend time with yourself, you must not be afraid to be alone. Knowing yourself is the beginning of all wisdom"
— Aristotle

ONCE YOU HAVE DEALT WITH the surprise that arises from finally seeing the toxicity in the people, there may be some blaming on your behalf. You might get critical of yourself for not noticing, being stupid, or whatever cruel label you want to slap on your forehead. That is not at all helpful or even appropriate; as I said before, you can't be objective sitting in the middle of subjective experience.

Discomfort motivates change and, because of the focus society places on families and friendship and love, we feel pressured to give that "one more chance". Before you know it, decades have passed. Also, up until the point that you finally saw the truth of your circumstances, you probably haven't stopped to consider your own experience of this relationship. You have been distracted by your need to impress them, earn their love, that you haven't noticed that there has been nothing coming back. On the odd occasion that you do notice, you simply interpret it as feedback of your shortcomings. The more we are exposed to toxic people, the higher our tolerance rises. If we are around people who tick all the toxic boxes, we will forgive what appears to be minor transgressions. These only appear minor because of the far worse behaviours we can be subjected to. This skews our perspective and allows abuse to go unacknowledged. So you haven't been bad or stupid: you have been human. In the middle of the chaos, the clues went unnoticed; now that you have seen them, you can do something about it.

Toxic people rarely enjoy your attempts at self-improvement. They want you right where you have always been, predicting and fulfilling their ever-increasing demands. They have no interest beyond their own needs and are unconcerned with your quality of life. You wanting to change is undeniably going to rock the boat. They have a choice: they can support you as you embark on this journey of discovery, or not. You then need to reflect on the quality of people you want in your life. Do you want people in your life who cannot support you and even go as far as to sabotage your life? (The right answer here is a) NO or b) HELL NO). I acknowledge it is difficult to accept the truth of their limitations. Once you have decided to empower yourself, you will slowly start to notice the impact of the toxic people in your life and the effect it has had on your self-esteem, your health (mental and physical) and all your relationship choices.

I will not lie to you: change is difficult and when you have been under the influence of toxic people for a long time, your confidence will be eroded to the point that you will second guess your decisions. There will be sadness, anger, regret, blame—you name it. That is all part of the process. You may find it difficult at first to celebrate your progress because you feel ashamed and uncomfortable about your health and wellbeing. In your efforts not to become a victim for a time, you might even find yourself using some of the old tried and true tricks your toxic teacher has taught you. After all, it is a defence mechanism, but the truth is that in a functioning, loving, respectful relationship, there is no need for defending.

Toxicity is dangerous and highly contagious. Often, if someone has upset our day we feel bad so we pass on the toxicity to the next person we come in contact with in the form of judgement or impatience. Just ask the next person who serves you at the local shops how many times they have weathered the wrath of a customer because they forgot to offer a bag for their chicken. They were simply in the wrong place at the wrong time. If they take it personally, that will spread the toxicity further as they take it home to their family and friends. The poison is unconsciously spread. Harm continues.

This is why removing toxic people from your life is critical to your survival. The lessons you have learned are invaluable if you use them as a catalyst for change and growth. If you buy into the abuse, it dims your light, shrinks your world, and your capacity to bloom.

"Man is not fully conditioned and determined
but rather determines himself whether he gives
in to conditions or stands up to them"
— Viktor E. Frankl

Caution: the following information is by no means advocating that you jump from a toxic relationship armed with your list and land straight into another one. There is a space that you need to occupy before moving on to a new relationship. That space is the space where you spend time on your relationship with yourself. This is a sacred time for healing and personal growth. It is also a space for integration. We can discover the reasons why we have lived our lives the way we have, forgive ourselves for the part we have played in all of our experiences, forgive others for also being human and intellectually embrace the new way forward BUT until we have fully integrated this new knowledge, we will repeat our old patterns when put under pressure.

So how do we fully integrate this new knowledge? Practice, practice, practice. Start small, using your voice and connecting with your truth in all exchanges with others. Become a sponge, soaking up all the tools and resources available to you. Write down all your unfulfilled dreams and desires and work out ways that you can make them happen (discard the ones that are on the list because you feel that is what is expected of you). Live the life you want to live, not the life you have been expected to live.

Use this time with yourself wisely—don't see it as a waiting room until something better happens. You are the person you are looking for! Finally, you can explore who you are and the mark you want to make on the world. Change doesn't have to be globally recognised or accompanied by big wads of cash to be significant. It can be as profound as changing the relationship with yourself and, in doing so, changing all the women in your family through your example. Demonstrating that the way things have been done in this family can be changed, and changed in a way that connects each of you with your innate wisdom and strength.

Question everything and everyone in your life up until this moment. Take an inventory of your relationships and see what adds and subtracts from the quality of your life. It is your right to be selective about who dwells in your inner circle. It is also okay to set boundaries and limit the time with those who are invested in keeping you where you have always been.

It's human nature to want or need to be part of a group. It is natural to feel apprehensive that, if we take that first step to make a change, assert our own needs and preferences, or reach for something we want, we may alienate our group and end up alone. Friends, family and partners can sometimes reinforce your fear by sabotaging your attempts to make improvements in your life that will give you less time with them, take you away from them, or potentially lead you to outgrow them. Well-intentioned, and because they love you and enjoy your company, they may encourage you to make decisions that keep you with them without considering the broader impact on your life.

Other times, people can consciously hold you back, acting on their fear of being alone, simple selfishness, control, or jealousy. In some families, nobody's happy unless everyone stays in their place and members will be threatened by your need to evolve. Some families believe the only way for the family to remain stable is for all members to keep their correct place (great idea—if you don't hold the position of the family doormat!). If you belong to such a family, you may challenge everyone's sense of security. They will feel compelled to quickly remind you of your place and demand that you get back to normal.

This kind of family loyalty is the worst kind of loyalty because membership to the family requires that nobody changes or grows. The mentality is that "if I can't get out of my situation, neither should you". I remember talking to a client who had left a domestic violence situation. She had confessed to her mother that she had left because of the violence, thinking that her mother (who had lived with her father's violent ways right until the day he died) would applaud her actions. Instead, her mother said, "the women in our family don't leave. We don't give up". Instead of joy, my client experienced great shame for breaking the code. A code that could have effectively killed her!

This is the space to exercise caution because the threat of losing our tribe can be so scary that we might sabotage ourselves to avoid testing the limits of our family. But if you have a dream for your life that is not being supported and you feel suffocated by the role your family has assigned to you, it might be time to fight your way out.

If people love you, they will want you to grow. If somebody doesn't want you to grow, you can call their feelings about you by many names, but you cannot call it love. You can call it fear, anger, control issues, resentment... but nobody has ever held anyone back because of love. Holding yourself back to make other people happy will not serve you and, ultimately, it will not serve them either. It is during this time that you can identify how you have acted in the same way towards others and called it "love" as you attempted to recreate the familiar behavioural patterns of your family.

When you have reached that place that you love yourself unconditionally, own all aspects of your life, are authentically, unapologetically yourself and don't keep people in your life because of a fear of being alone, you have graduated to a place where you don't need anyone else in your life to complete you. Only when you have permitted yourself to outgrow your family role and have developed new healthy relationships will you be ready for a new healthy romantic relationship.

So back to the list. This is what a healthy relationship looks like:

- Your friends, your partner share your basic values and life goals.
- You all know what you want out of life, what your common goals are, what you wish to accomplish in life, and are firmly committed to achieving these together.
- You trust each other and can safely and openly discuss everything that impacts you. The good, the bad, and the ugly. There are no secrets from the past or the present.
- You keep your own identity and so do your friends and partner. You don't transform yourself to please others. You remain true to you.
- You spend quality time together doing things that are mutually fulfilling as well as quality time apart doing what is important to you individually.
- You encourage each other to grow and change. You aren't threatened by each other's growth; you are

happy that you can be a part of their becoming a better person.

- It is safe to communicate your needs and wants, whether it be in the bedroom or any other room in the house. You set aside time to discuss the issues relevant to you as a couple or individually. You know that you are being listened to and that it is okay to check for understanding.

- You can agree to disagree because you respect each other's differences, even if you disagree on important issues. You always seek a fair compromise.

- Your relationship expectations are realistic. You focus on what will add value to the quality of your shared lives.

- Each of you contributes your fair share to the relationship by dividing the fun and not so fun responsibilities equally between you.

- Both of you respect each other's family ties and friendships. While it's important to set aside time for family and friends, it's also important to maintain healthy boundaries between you and your partner as a unit apart from other close relationships.

A truly loving relationship is caring, kind, supportive, encouraging, and empathetic. There is no room for the toxic behaviours previously mentioned. Boundaries are respected. A healthy relationship is built on the desire to complement each other, not complete each other.

Let Go

"Between stimulus and response, there is a space. In that space is our power to choose our response. In our response lies our growth and our freedom"
— Viktor E. Frankl

YOUR LIFE TO THIS POINT may not have left you with the knowledge of just how truly magnificent you are. I am sorry for that. That's not fair. What it is... is life. None of us are born into perfect families or get to live a life without the unexpected challenging us and our family units and that's okay. When we accept the imperfections of our families and ourselves, our circumstances, and the rights of others to be equally imperfect change, positive change can happen.

It is hanging on to what is extremely damaging to us by refusing to acknowledge the truth of our experience that will cause us the greatest harm. We are no longer children filled with magic that can heal the world. We are adults and, if we truly want to make the world a better place, we need to start with making ourselves better.

We can let go of our need for people to acknowledge just how bad our story is and instead be honest with ourselves. We can acknowledge that a bully is nothing without a victim—and we can stop being a victim. We can comprehend the power in choice and choose to choose better options for ourselves. We can choose to stop taking responsibility for anyone else's behaviour but our own. We can revel in the freedom and opportunities that open up to us when we connect with the power available to us as adults. As children, we were dependent, vulnerable, and powerless; as adults this is only the case if we choose to make it so. If you didn't know that, there is no need to be upset. I sincerely believe that all that we need turns up in our lives when we are ready to receive. You weren't ready, but now you are. Don't waste a moment of it by swimming in a pond full of "shoulds".

It is time, my friend. I am handing over to you two words that will unlock that damn cage forever. *Let go*. I'm not telling you to pretend the past didn't happen. I am not asking you to pretend that you weren't hurt or, if there are people who did bad things, that you don't hold them accountable. I am telling you to let go of the thinking that no longer serves you, the lies you believed about yourself, and the self-destructive relationships you have held on to for far too long. Let go of those emotions that you have repressed forever and the need to be what you think other people need to see. Let go of the belief that you are not enough. I don't have to meet you to know that isn't true; it never was. It is time to love yourself up to the wazoo!

- It is our job to draw a line in the sand and decide that change will happen.

- It is our job to heal that which has intentionally and unintentionally bruised our souls.
- It is our job to create our reality based on love, respect, and self-validation.
- It is our job to choose our support crew through this process.
- It is our job to set goals, dream in colour and realise our potential.
- It is our job to surrender the hope that is harming us.
- It is our job to throw open the door of our self-imposed cage, yelling "I have arrived!"

Don't feel burdened by it being your job; rejoice! Your life, your safety and your heart is finally in the hands of someone that knows you—all of you—and that person now knows just what they need to do give you the love you always deserved.

"The meaning of life is to give life meaning"
— Viktor E. Frankl

I am not going to wish you luck because luck has no place in this discussion. I am not going to lie to you: habits are hard to break. You will need a strong resolve and dogged determination to let go of the familiarity of your story because, strangely, it feels comfortable. Yes, we humans are strange creatures; we like to stay in places we know, even if it hurts like hell.

Your story—like all core beliefs, all safety behaviours—serves a purpose, giving you the tools you need ensure the support of the people that matter to you. Your story is hardwired; once it feels the threat of you trying to modify it, it will resist. It will call your name often with all its might, tempting you back to the arms of the familiar but self-destructive. Be strong. You will need to resist.

You have all that you need to not answer that call. The strength you deny you have exists within you already—you simply haven't realised it. Your strength and resilience have sustained you and fuelled you, allowing you to get up day after day while you took the punishment and tried to be good enough to earn love. It takes great strength to try again and again, hanging onto hope. So you have the skills under your belt; you just haven't been using them in the way that makes you feel good. Now you can use that strength to turn up for yourself!

Wake up each morning embracing the opportunities ahead of you. Be grateful for the opportunity, the breath you draw into your lungs, the experience that bought you here, and move your gaze to the future. Permit yourself to look back only to remind yourself of why you have taken this new direction and promise yourself you will never again visit the past to shame yourself. Wrap your arms around yourself, fill your heart with self-forgiveness and take in a deep life-affirming breath because you have the best kind of work to do.

You are not alone. Know that there is help out there in those times that you feel overwhelmed by the choices in front of you. Being brave doesn't mean that this has to be a solo journey. Being brave is being vulnerable and connecting with those who can walk by your side as you embark on this adventure.

· It is never too late to choose you.
· It is never too late to answer your soul's calling.
· It is never too late to fulfil your destiny.
· It is never too late.

Now is the time to let go of that which no longer serves you. Now is the time to become the person you choose to be, not the person you were programmed to be. Now is the time to bust out of the cage called hope; you have suffered enough.

It's time and you know it.

With unconditional love for all versions of you,
Shelley

About Shelley

Shelley Murphy

Counsellor & Psychotherapist

Master of Counselling & Psychotherapy UofA

Member of the ACA College of Supervisors

Member of the ACA College of Clinical Counsellors

Level 4 Member Australian Counselling Association

I have worked as a therapist in private practice since 2008 after taking a redundancy package from a large corporation. When I left that role, I vowed to never again work somewhere that didn't make my heart sing. In pursuit of that goal, during the final years of my corporate employment, I finally realised a life-long dream and became a uni student. I studied part-time until I received my golden handshake and I completed my study as a full-time student.

During this time, I started volunteering with women experiencing homelessness, which led to my employment with that organisation. The study bug hadn't left me, so I applied to the Masters of Counselling and Psychotherapy programme at Adelaide University as a full-time student. My passion is helping others to achieve their best life.

Since 2017, I have worked with my life partner to assist people with overcoming anxiety. We are a mobile service and travel to our clients' homes in the Adelaide area, running sessions online for our friends interstate and overseas. I am blessed that I get to work with my best friend and witness inspirational moments daily.

Contact

Email: Counsellor@outlook.com.au
Phone: 0407 435 169
Web: AdelaideAnxietyTherapy.com
https://www.facebook.com/ShelleyMurphyCounselling/

Bibliography

Allen, E., & Bird, M. (2020). The Value of Vulnerability in Relationships. Family Perspectives, 1(1): 7. https://scholarsarchive.byu.edu/familyperspectives/vol1/iss1/7

Arbel, R, Schacter, H. L., Kazmierski, K. F. M., Daspe, M-È & Margolin, G. (2018). Adverse childhood experiences, daily worries, and positive thoughts: A daily diary multi-wave study. British Journal of Clinical Psychology, 57(4) 514–519. https://doi.org/10.1111/bjc.12200

Asmundson, G. J. G., & Afif, T. (2019). Adverse Childhood Experiences: Using evidence to advance research, practice, policy, and prevention. Academic Press.

Australian Early Development Census (n.d.). Brain development in children. https://www.aedc.gov.au/resources/resources-accessible/brain-development-in-children

Australian Institute of Health and Welfare. (n.d). Family, domestic and sexual violence. https://www.aihw.gov.au/reports-data/behaviours-risk-factors/domestic-violence/overview

Beck Institute for Cognitive Behavior Therapy. (n.d.). Core Beliefs Archives. https://beckinstitute.org/tag/core-beliefs/

Bowlby, J. (1988). A secure base: parent-child attachment and healthy human development. Basic Books.

Bowlby, J. (1997). Attachment and Loss, Vol. 1: Attachment. Pimlico.

Bowlby, J. (1998). Attachment and Loss, Vol. 2: Separation: Anger and anxiety. Pimlico.

BrainyQuote. (n.d.). Friedrich Nietzsche Quotes. https://www.brainyquote.com/quotes/friedrich_nietzsche_105845 [

Brown, B. (2010, June). The power of vulnerability [Video]. TEDxHouston. https://www.ted.com/talks/brene_brown_the_power_of_vulnerability

Department of Social Services, Australian Government. (n.d.). Women's Safety. https://www.dss.gov.au/our-responsibilities/womens-safety

Feuerman, M. (2017, February 24). Your Attachment Style Influences the Success of Your Relationship. The Gottman Institute. https://www.gottman.com/blog/attachment-style-influences-success-relationship/

Lerner, H. G. (1990). The dance of intimacy: A woman's guide to courageous acts of change in key relationships. Harper Perennial.

Lerner, H. G. (2001). The dance of deception: A guide to authenticity and truth-telling in women's relationships. Quill.

Lerner, H. G. (2005). The dance of fear: Rising above anxiety, fear, and shame to be your best and bravest self. Perennial Currents.

Lerner, H. G. (2014). The dance of anger: A woman's guide to changing the patterns of intimate relationships. William Morrow & Co.

Lerner, H. G. (2018). Why won't you apologize?: Healing big betrayals and everyday hurts. Duckworth Overlook.

Lifeline Australia. (2016). Lifeline Australia - 13 11 14 - Crisis Support and Suicide Prevention. https://www.lifeline.org.au/

Lowell, A., Renk, K., & Adgate, A. H. (2014). The role of attachment in the relationship between child maltreatment and later emotional and behavioral functioning. Child Abuse & Neglect, 38(9), 1436-1449. https://doi.org/10.1016/j.chiabu.2014.02.006.

MensLine Australia. (n.d.). Experiencing Violence. https://mensline.org.au/family-violence/experiencing-violence/

Moore, T. (2006). Early Childhood And Long Term Development: The Importance of the Early Years. Australian Research Alliance for Children and Youth. https://www.aracy.org.au/publications-resources/command/download_file/id/97/filename/Early_childhood_and_long_term_development_-_The_importance_of_the_early_years.pdf

Nietzsche, F., Faber, M., & Lehmann, S. (2004). Human, all too human. Penguin.

Omri, G., Karantzas, G. C., & Fraley, R. C. (2016). Adult Attachment. Academic Press. https://doi.org/10.1016/B978-0-12-420020-3.00002-5.

On the Line. (n.d.). Helplines for men's mental health, men's help & counselling. https://ontheline.org.au/mental-health-helplines/mens-mental-and-social-health/

Osmo, F., Duran, V., Wenzel, A., Reis de Oliveira, I., Nepomuceno, S., Madeira, M., & Menezes, I. (2018). The Negative Core Beliefs Inventory: Development and Psychometric Properties. Journal of Cognitive Psychotherapy, 32(1), 67–84. http://eprints.lincoln.ac.uk/id/eprint/31173/2/31173%20accepted%20JCP-32-1-00005_print.pdf.

Pérez, V. R., & Martínez, L. M. R. (2015). Attachment, fear, coping strategies and intra-family relationships in children. Psychology and Health, 25(1), 91–101. http://psicologiaysalud.uv.mx/index.php/psicysalud/article/view/1342

Pope, A. (2019). An Essay on Man: Epistle I. Poetry Foundation. https://www.poetryfoundation.org/poems/44899/an-essay-on-man-epistle-i.

Psych Central. (2018). Children and Grief. https://psychcentral.com/lib/children-and-grief/

Siegel, D.J. (2020). Developing Mind: How relationships and the brain interact to shape who we are. Guilford.

Siegel, D.J. (2012). Pocket guide to interpersonal neurobiology: An integrative handbook of the mind. W.W. Norton.

Stamateas, B. (2012). Emotional wounds: Healing the past for a better tomorrow. B de Bolsillo.

Suicide Call Back Service. (2017). Mental health counselling & suicide prevention. https://www.suicidecallbackservice.org.au/.

TheFreeDictionary.com. (2019). hope. https://www.thefreedictionary.com/hope

The Gottman Institute. (2019). Reclaiming Our Stories From Trauma. https://www.gottman.com/blog/reclaiming-our-stories-from-trauma/

The National Domestic Violence Hotline. (2013). Abuse Defined. https://www.thehotline.org/is-this-abuse/abuse-defined/.

Valiente, R. M., Sandín, B., & Chorot, P. (2002). Common fears in children and adolescents: Relationship with sensitivity to anxiety, anxiety trait, negative affectivity and depression. Journal of Psychopathology and Clinical Psychology, 7 (1), 61–70. http://revistas.uned.es/index.php/RPPC/article/view/3922

1800respect.org.au. (2016). Healthy relationships. https://www.1800respect.org.au/healthy-relationships/.

Lightning Source UK Ltd.
Milton Keynes UK
UKHW010058291220
375862UK00002B/558